PENGUIN BOOKS

GROW RICH
with the
PROPERTY CYCLE

Kieran Trass has worked in property for two decades as an investor, financier and advisor. He runs his own property investment group of companies, Hybrid Group, specialising in residential property investment. Kieran was a founding committee member of the Auckland Property Investors Association in 1994 and is a past secretary of the New Zealand Property Investors Federation.

He has spent some years specifically studying the property market and has made some startling observations on the predictability of the property cycle.

GROW RICH

with the

PROPERTY CYCLE

Kieran Trass

PENGUIN BOOKS

PENGUIN BOOKS
Published by the Penguin Group
Penguin Group (NZ), cnr Airborne and Rosedale Roads, Albany,
Auckland 1310, New Zealand
Penguin Books Ltd, 80 Strand, London, WC2R 0RL, England
Penguin Group (USA) Inc., 375 Hudson Street, New York, NY 10014, United States
Penguin Group (Australia), 250 Camberwell Road, Camberwell,
Victoria 3124, Australia
Penguin Books Canada Ltd, 10 Alcorn Avenue, Toronto,
Ontario, Canada M4V 3B2
Penguin Books (South Africa) (Pty) Ltd, 24 Sturdee Avenue, Rosebank,
Johannesburg 2196, South Africa
Penguin Books India (P) Ltd, 11, Community Centre, Panchsheel Park,
New Delhi 110 017, India
Penguin Ireland Ltd, 25 St Stephen's Green, Dublin 2, Ireland
Penguin Books Ltd, Registered Offices: 80 Strand, London, WC2R 0RL, England

First published by Penguin Group (NZ), 2004
1 3 5 7 9 10 8 6 4 2

Copyright Kieran Trass 2004

The right of Kieran Trass to be identified as the author of this work in terms of
section 96 of the Copyright Act 1994 is hereby asserted.

Designed and Typeset by Egan-Reid Ltd
Printed in Australia by McPherson's Printing Group

ISBN 0-14-301943-0
A catalogue record for this book is available
from the National Library of New Zealand.
www.penguin.co.nz

Contents

Foreword

The recent upsurge in property value has only served to fuel the desire to own investment property, and increasing numbers of people have joined the residential rental investment market. However, blind faith in real estate as a stable investment with assured growth is misguided. Most investors make careful calculations based on conservative growth assumptions relating to net cashflow and capital appreciation over the projected holding period. Such calculations enhance judgment and allow comparison with other asset classes. In the recent heady times, seminars designed to guide this process have sprung up and it has become almost trendy to attend at least one offering. There has always been a plethora of books outlining methods of analysing properties and illustrating how inevitable uncertainties, assumptions and opinions can be rationalised into effective decision-making processes.

This book is fascinating, because it offers the investor another tool that stands alongside analysis of the individual property and as such is unique and invaluable. By taking a new look at the natural movement that occurs within the property market over time, Kieran Trass reveals the answer to the perennial question of 'when is it the right time to buy and sell?' To the principle strands of the property investment decision – choice of an appropriate property, payment of the right price, and selection of appropriate finance – he adds 'action at the correct time'. This book provides straightforward pointers to understanding the 'windows of opportunity' that happen at times during movement of the property clock, and are critical factors to overwhelming success and wealth creation.

I first met Kieran when I invited him to the university to speak to a second-year property class. He was an instant success. His enthusiasm and knowledge of investment property stems from first-hand experience and powerful business acumen. He has a way of explaining property investment techniques that make plain sense and offer real practical tools for success. This book will give you a real advantage; I recommend it to you as I do to my students.

Susan Flint-Hartle
Senior Lecturer in Property
Massey University
Auckland

Introduction

The concept of the property cycle is a relatively modern one and because it seems complex it is often avoided altogether by property authors. After more than twenty years observing the property cycle in action in New Zealand and helping clients accumulate property as well as creating my own riches from property investment, I have certainly learned a lot about the property cycle. This book is the culmination of what I have gained from research, experience and observing thousands of other investors' experiences in this very specialised field. It will teach you the basic principles of the property cycle and how you can use them to grow rich or accumulate wealth.

I recently made a comment at a public seminar and someone in the audience called out, 'But Kieran, that's just your opinion!' He was right, of course, and I said, 'You are correct, the ideas, theories, thoughts, concepts and advice I give you tonight are all based on my own opinion and experiences. That opinion is based on over twenty years' experience in the finance industry, and over ten years analysing thousands of property investors' portfolios and helping other property investors finance and grow their portfolios as well as actively investing in residential property myself.'

Needless to say the gentleman who had made the remark replied with a simple, 'Fair enough.' While my opinions may not be acceptable to everyone, they are not formed lightly and are qualified by my depth of experience within the field of property investment.

New Zealand is often considered an ideal place to test new products and services as it is a free, democratic market with little government intervention and one where consumer demand rules. The theory is that if something new works well in the tiny New Zealand market, then it can do exceptionally well in a similar but much larger market. So too the study of New Zealand's property cycle gives a good insight into how property cycles operate else-where, and the lessons learned can be applied in much larger centres around the world where the free market also generally rules and demand is driven by consumers.

'. . . this book is not designed to convince you
to invest in property . . .'

This book is divided into four sections.

The first provides an overview of the main factors that drive the property cycle and describes the emotions of fear and greed that occur throughout the cycle. You will learn why the property cycle is so predictable, and how to read the property cycle clock so you can follow the progress of your local property market. You will also learn to differentiate between the *key drivers* of the property cycle and the lesser impacting factors called *market influencers*.

The second section looks at the three stages of each phase of the property cycle (boom, slump and recovery) and outlines the clues provided during each stage by the media, as well as investors' likely reactions during each phase of the cycle based on their fear and greed. Section two will give an insight into the strategies utilised by wise property investors in the various phases of the property cycle.

Section three shows how you can secure your financial health regardless of the impacts of the various phases of the property cycle and answers the age-old question, 'When is it a good time to buy property?'

Section four explains the critical finance cycles, which are implicitly linked to the real estate cycle, and also considers whether the property cycle is now an obsolete concept.

Acknowledgements

This book is written for the benefit of all property investors including the past, present and future clients of the Hybrid Group of companies. Sincere thanks and appreciation go to all those people who have shared their property experiences with me and to those from whom I have had the opportunity to learn over the years. You have contributed a vast range of experiences to my real estate knowledge.

My sincere appreciation is also due to my wife, Jo, for sacrificing some of our date nights and for your consistent and unwavering belief in, and support for, me. You mean more to me than I can express in mere words.

A special thanks goes to Steve McMenemy (particularly for all those Saturday morning efforts), and Taylor and Anthony for helping me 'keep it real!' Your collective inspiration and encouragement has often given me strength when I have needed it most.

My family and close friends deserve thanks for your unbelievable level of understanding and tolerance of my sometimes fanatical attitude to my businesses and property investment activities. My parents particularly deserve recognition for accidentally teaching me how easy it is to create wealth from property. As I grew up I saw them make huge sacrifices by adding value to the properties we lived in. As a result they created some wealth and then unselfishly used that wealth to give our family better opportunities and a better lifestyle. Thanks Mum and Dad. Words fail to express my gratitude for all you have done.

My co-workers have given me fantastic input and demonstrated a fun attitude to what many people might call work. You know that I am always open to changing my mind if I am given a good enough reason. So keep challenging me, as I always welcome your opinions.

Appreciation also goes to the economists at Infometrics for providing much of the raw data and graphs used in this book.

Finally I wish to acknowledge Homer Hoyt, whom I consider to be the grandfather of the concept of the property cycle. Homer wrote about the basic concept in 1933 and some of his insights into the property cycle have proved remarkably relevant even to this day.

PART 1

The Property Cycle

Chapter 1

What is the Property Cycle?

This book is designed to teach you how to create your own property investment riches by using the property cycle to your financial advantage. Property investment is not a get-rich-quick scheme although at times during the property cycle you can accumulate significant wealth relatively quickly. The phrase 'grow rich' was chosen for the title of this book rather than 'get rich' because it takes time to accumulate sustainable wealth from the property cycle. Many property investors are not interested in taking their time to get rich and are constantly seeking the latest shortcut to wealth. The smartest property investors understand that property investment is not a get-rich scheme but rather a grow-rich strategy.

So what is the property cycle?

Definition of the Property Cycle

'An irregular but recurrent and predictable succession of causes and effects that the property market experiences with resultant impacts on the creation and destruction of property wealth.'

In my many years involved in property investment there is one question I have been asked over and over again, irrespective of whether property prices are increasing, decreasing or remaining stable. This question seems to be the one everyone interested in property investment wants answered: 'Is now the right time to invest in property?' It probably comes as no surprise to you because you too have always wanted to know the answer.

I have long held the opinion that it is always the right time to buy if you buy right! However the persistence of the question above led me to question whether there *was* an optimum time to buy property or optimum times to use specific property investment strategies. This led to my study of whether a property cycle existed.

The property cycle is the term used to describe a succession of similar events that affect the property market on a cyclical basis. By understanding the property cycle, you can get an insight into why the property market reacts the way it does. You will learn how you can use the property cycle to your financial advantage and which investment strategies are likely to produce better results during the specific phases of the cycle. Many intelligent investors have failed to use the property cycle to their advantage. This appears to be due to the powerful emotions of fear and greed that are evident throughout the cycle, causing investors to react emotionally without even realising it.

When I first began studying the concept of a property cycle I almost did not want to believe that it existed, or if it did, that it might be predictable. I thought that if a property cycle existed and could be predicted, then surely more people would have already used it to their financial advantage and the secret would already be out! To my pleasant surprise I found enough evidence to conclude that the property cycle clearly does exist. It has some immutable aspects, is measurable and is quite predictable. I also gained some insight into why more people do not use it to their advantage.

While the progress of the property cycle is predictable, it is not an exact science. Determining the future trends of the many key drivers of the property cycle is difficult, as there are so many other influencing factors that can impact upon them. However my research indicates that these key drivers do tend to follow a regular pattern and reach peaks of activity at specific phases of the property cycle. Therefore if you consider the property cycle as a whole, you can learn why and when these key drivers typically peak and the resultant impact they have on the property cycle. There is no crystal ball here and no new ideas, but rather a new combination of existing information to help you as a property investor achieve a glimpse of what lies ahead for your property investment fortunes.

There is every indication that the same property cycle exists in any country's residential property market where supply and demand are driven by a free market combined with a deregulated finance industry without significant intervention from political or government forces. If the finance industry is either underdeveloped or overly protected by regulation, then imbalance or volatility can interfere with the underlying property cycle's progress. Historically when countries have deregulated their finance industry at the same time as having favourable tax law for property investment, a property price bubble has occurred and resulted in a subsequent significant correction in property values.

The Three Phases of the Property Cycle

There is much confusion about the property cycle, often caused by sensational media reporting, which gives rise to differing opinions as to whether or not property is a sound investment vehicle.

The property cycle has sometimes been interpreted as including a number of phases ranging from a property bust to a property boom. However when you look at the historical performance of the property market, it becomes clear that the cycle consists of only three major phases.

The property cycle consistently and repetitively experiences these three distinct phases during each complete cycle. I have labelled these three phases *boom*, *slump* and *recovery*.

I will use the illustration of the property cycle clock to describe the property cycle throughout this book. (For more detail on the property cycle clock see Chapter 3.)

PROPERTY CYCLE CLOCK ®

Where in the World Does the Property Cycle Exist?

Whether you are investing in New Zealand, the UK, Ireland, Australia, the USA, Sweden, Norway, Finland or even in parts of Asia, the same basic property cycle can be seen historically. These simple patterns have been particularly strong since the mid-1980s when financial deregulation occurred in many of these countries. The property cycle can often become exaggerated and prolonged by larger populations causing sustained rises or declines in either the supply of property or the demand for property. This is probably a result of the greater momentum created by larger populations.

Irrespective of a population's size, the property cycle can be volatile. This volatility can result in property values oscillating significantly (Graph 1.1). There have been periods when property values decreased so far that a significant portion of the population have had negative equity in their property (that is, when the owner owes more than the curent value of the property). This situation occurred in the early 1990s in New Zealand and the UK.

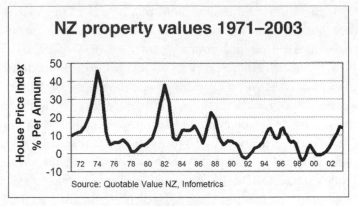

Graph 1.1

There are some country-specific influencers on property markets throughout the world (for example the treatment of issues such as depreciation and capital gains) which can exaggerate the effects on property values, but the property cycle follows the same basic progression regardless of these influencers. (For more details on market influencers see Chapter 6.)

The New Zealand property cycle offers an excellent model to study as New Zealand has a largely deregulated property and finance industry. This means that the free market reigns for property values, and consequently the property cycle operates efficiently from an economic perspective. New Zealand is also a relatively small economy so its property cycles tend to be shorter than those of larger economies. This makes the study of the causes and effects of the various forces driving the property cycle relatively easy to identify.

While the concept of the property cycle is not a recent discovery, little research on property cycles had been undertaken internationally prior to 1980. Today there is widespread acknowledgement that property cycles exist and much debate over whether or not future property cycles can be predicted. My research indicates that property cycles are predictable as they follow a basic pattern. This pattern was discovered over seventy years ago by the grandfather of the property cycle concept, an American by the name of Homer Hoyt. In his book *100 Years of Land Values in Chicago*, written in 1933,[1] he analyses the movement of Chicago's land values, and notes that a recurrent succession of causes and effects impacted on these values during the hundred years from 1830 to 1930.

Hoyt concluded that a property cycle certainly existed, and identified some of its consistent key drivers. He noted that key drivers such as population growth often initially created increased demand for property. Increased demand was followed by a sharp rise in rents, which resulted in increased land values because of the greater financial returns available from buildings. Hoyt then observed significant increases in the construction of new buildings as a result of higher margins being achieved by construction firms. Finally, too much new construction produced an oversupply of property that eventually resulted in rent reductions and subsequent property price erosion. This pattern is still in evidence in property markets today, and is possibly even more apparent due to the ready availability and quality of statistical data now available.

The more you invest in residential property, the more critical it becomes to understand the property cycle. It surprises me that even experienced investors sometimes get caught out by the property cycle and end up losing much, if not all, of their property wealth. History is littered with examples of formerly successful property investors who have suffered huge losses as a result of not paying attention to the property cycle and by falling victim to their own fear or greed.

A good example of this was a client of a bank I worked for in Auckland, New Zealand. The Auckland property market had experienced a peak in a property boom, property values seemed to stall, and inflation halved in a relatively short space of time. Banks were concerned that some clients might be over-extended and over-exposed to what suddenly looked like a fragile property market. The head office of this particular bank ordered a review of clients who had large property portfolios. One client had his entire property portfolio revalued, and as a result the bank was no longer comfortable with his level of exposure to the property market. He had bought many properties over a long period of time using the equity he had in his property portfolio, until he had close to twenty investment properties. But the bank systematically forced the sale of the majority of his portfolio to reduce their risk, even though he had never defaulted on any loan repayments. He was almost wiped out financially as a result, with the last of his investment properties sold by the bank just before the property market moved into the recovery phase of the next property cycle. This investor got caught out by the property cycle. If he had understood the way it worked, he would have known how to recognise where the market was in relation to the property cycle and that a boom period was not the wisest time to aggressively grow his portfolio. He could well have retained a smaller portfolio and still owned it if he had understood the concept of the property cycle.

Is the Property Cycle Different this Time?

The property cycle plays a critical role in any strategy to create wealth through property investment.

In recent property booms all around the world, the most common argument as to why property prices are not overvalued is that the current internationally low interest rate environment allows people to borrow more. The argument is that as a result of lower interest rates, investors and homeowners are willing to pay more for property – therefore higher property prices are justified. But what about the fundamental investment principle of return on investment? Surely property prices should simply reflect their return on investment or, to put it another way, the income stream a property might generate? Ardent promoters of property as an investment vehicle will argue that 'things are different this time', and usually raise two main points against the requirement for an adequate return on investment.

1. They will point out that property prices are driven not only by a need for a return on investment, but also because people own property for their own use, as a home to live in. The

theory is that any return on investment is irrelevant to property as an asset class for these purchasers. While true enough in essence the difficulty with this claim is twofold. First, those buying their own home still only have limited financial resources, and any extra funds they need to borrow to buy their home will have a detrimental impact on their lifestyle choices as the repayment of extra borrowings will reduce their surplus cashflow. Secondly, during a boom a large percentage of property sales are actually made to investors, who subsequently lead the market and drive property values even higher. Those purchasing their own homes simply follow the price leaders, who as investors are often prepared to accept lower returns in light of lower interest rates.

2. They will claim that any return forecast from property really should include a component for future capital growth, thereby justifying a much higher value than is acceptable based purely on rental returns. But what other investment vehicle relies on capital growth to justify its purchase price? When you invest in shares, do you make investment decisions by basing the purchase price of those shares on any expected capital growth of those shares? There have been periods when this *was* the case, such as prior to the crash of 1987 and the dot.com crash of 2000; but these events ended with huge captial losses! It is true that property is very different from shares, which can become totally worthless whereas property always retains some value, but tell that to the owners of Japanese property who were wiped out financially in the 1990s. Because property can be highly leveraged, a small decrease in its value can effectively result in negative equity. Shares don't have that downside, and even margin trading of shares usually only results in the loss of your initial investment and no more. While projecting property's capital growth has its merits, these projections should not be relied upon to replace any expected short-to-medium-term return on investment.

Wise investors have often heard the catch-cry 'But this time it's different because . . .' to justify why a current boom should last longer than ever before. But they understand that the basic principles of the property cycle always remain the same and many have used this knowledge to increase their financial net worth while minimising their investment risks. The property cycle provides many telltale clues that clearly indicate what is in store for the property market.

As you read this book you will learn that the property cycle has a distinct and predictable progression, and you will also learn how the property cycle impacts on property values as it progresses. You will come to realise that the property cycle is a complex topic, but not as complex as it first may seem – and that it is well worth the effort to understand.

Using the property cycle to my own advantage as an investor has enabled me to secure significant wealth in remarkably short periods of time. Just one example of this is a property I purchased in central Auckland, New Zealand, in November 2001 for $615,000. This increased in value by over 40% in less than two years, purely as a result of the property cycle. The rental income generated from this property also increased by over 30% during the same time. Its purchase was no coincidence but rather a calculated decision based on my knowledge of the local property market in relation to the property cycle. My recognition of the potential for a property boom in New Zealand in 2002 was publicly announced in the media before most property investors even realised a boom was coming. I write this not for the purpose of impressing you, but to impress *upon* you the potential value of understanding the property cycle.

'No doubt each new property cycle will bring new lessons, but the basic property cycle repeats the same pattern again and again because it is subject to a combination of key drivers which affect supply and demand of property.'

Once you understand the property cycle, you will be able to max-imise your returns from property investing while at the same time reducing your risk. You also need to understand why the property cycle occurs and how the cycle unleashes the powerful emotional forces of fear and greed in the property market. The keys to under-standing these matters are contained within this book.

The Property Cycle in Action

As I have already stated, the property cycle is predictable, but it is not an exact science. Some people believe history never repeats, but I am not convinced. I believe historical property cycles can give us some insight into what may be in store in the future.

The following graphs show the distinct pattern of the property cycle in several different countries from the mid- to late 1980s and throughout the 1990s. They reveal varying degrees of property price growth, but the three distinct stages of the property cycle can still be seen in each country. (Of course there are also local property cycles within the major cities and regions of each country, but for the purpose of this overview I have considered the property cycles of these countries as a whole.)

You will observe that the most extreme house price growth is recorded in the UK (Graph 1.2) and Australia (Graph 1.3) during the late 1980s when house price inflation peaked in those countries at around 35% per annum. Both of these countries then experienced a long slump phase.

In contrast, the USA (Graph 1.4) and New Zealand (Graph 1.5) experienced lower house price growth at their peaks in the late 1980s, followed by a much shorter slump phase in both of these countries compared with the UK and Australia.

While the data are not sufficient to draw a strong conclusion, it appears that periods of *very strong house price growth may well result in an extended slump phase.*

I have considered whether the duration of any specific phase has any consistent influence on the duration of a subsequent phase, but have found no clear evidence that this is the case. Certainly, over the

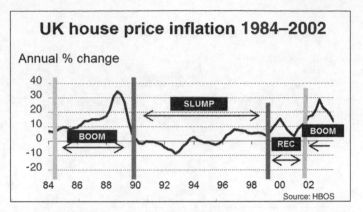

Graph 1.2

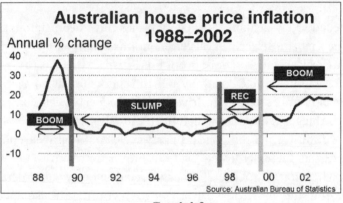

Graph 1.3

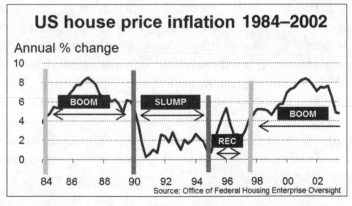

Graph 1.4

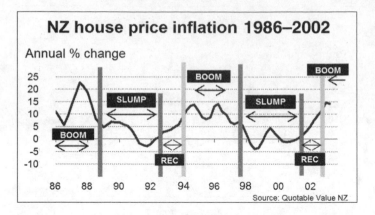

Graph 1.5

last decade New Zealand's property cycles have been significantly shorter than those seen in larger economies such as the UK, USA and Australia. I have no hard proof but I suspect this has to do with New Zealand's nimble economy which reacts quickly to a combination of changes in the key drivers of the property cycle compared with the bigger economies which have a much greater momentum.

The duration of a complete property cycle has not proved consistent, but has typically lasted for anything from seven to eighteen years. The longevity of each property cycle obviously varies depending on the state of the key drivers for each country. It also appears that a smaller economy such as New Zealand can experience faster cycles, and this may well be due to the increased volatility and limited inertia of the key drivers of the property cycle in smaller economies.

It is interesting to consider the time lapse between booms and slumps so I have graphed these below. Some useful observations are the long durations between the peak of one boom to that of the next boom, and the durations between the troughs of one slump and the next slump.

But the most interesting observation of all must be the relatively short duration between the peak of a boom and the trough of a slump which follows.

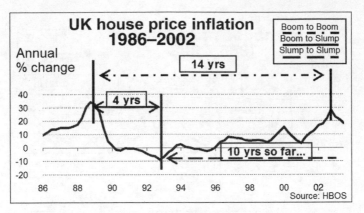

Graph 1.6

Graph 1.7

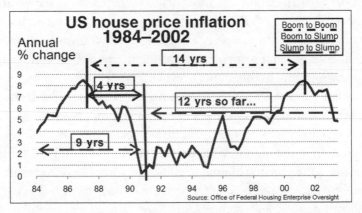

Graph 1.8

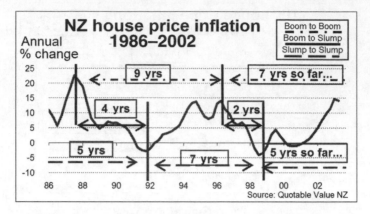

Graph 1.9

Are There Exceptions to the Property Cycle?

Just like everything in life there are a few exceptions to the rules of the property cycle, but these do not apply to the market as a whole.

There can be some properties within a city or region that continue to command a premium irrespective of what is happening to the property cycle. These properties are likely to have some sort of serious 'X' factor. Perhaps they have some historical significance or a combination of uniquely superior attributes, for example the best properties situated in the best locations of the best streets in the best suburbs of a city. There are numerous reasons why specific properties may defy the property cycle, but usually these reasons stem from the properties having unique features which render them largely immune to the property cycle.

Another exception is the emergence of specific localised hot spots, regardless of a city's or region's property cycle. These hot spots can defy the property cycle's impact on property prices in the region in which they are situated. Reasons for such hot spots emerging include the re-zoning of land to allow more intense developments to be constructed (therefore effectively increasing land values), or significant new projects being planned for an area. Such new projects can include new infrastructure resulting in the creation of numerous employment opportunities, or a significant increase in the level of public amenities available. Eventually though, these hot spots will be subject to the property cycle because they will reach a level of relativity to surrounding or similar locations.

A good example of this was in one of the southernmost parts of New Zealand, the city of Invercargill. The area suffered declining property values for many years as young people left the town for better employment opportunities. Then the decision was made to offer free tertiary education courses there, in sharp contrast to the large expense faced by students at any other educational institution in New Zealand. Of course, the subsequent impact on property values had little to do with the property cycle and everything to do with free education attracting droves of students into Invercargill! But this doesn't mean that property values there will continue to increase indefinitely. Values have certainly undergone a significant upward adjustment since the free education was offered, but eventually property values will find their equilibrium and then follow the property cycle once more.

Equally there can be a negative divergence from a city or region's property cycle creating cold spots, for example if new projects are abandoned or existing large employers in an area downsize, close down or relocate. Again this tends to be the exception rather than the rule.

Exceptions emerge as a result of culture shifts driven by lifestyle demands. The impact on property values can be positive, negative, or both. An example of such a culture shift could be baby boomers either seeking new lifestyle opportunities or abandoning previous lifestyles. This could increase property values in favoured new lifestyle locations and reduce property values in the former locations. Again, such exceptions to the property cycle will eventually complete their adjustment to the culture shift and will then follow the property cycle once again.

Such hot spots or cold spots typically emerge due to abnormal levels of demand created by a financially empowered or disempowered niche.

CHAPTER SUMMARY

- The property cycle is an irregular but recurrent and predictable succession of causes and effects experienced by the property market which results in the creation and destruction of property wealth.

- Historical evidence shows that the property cycle consistently passes through three distinct phases: boom, slump and recovery.

- The same phases of the cycle exist whether you are investing in New Zealand, the UK, Ireland, Australia, the USA, Sweden, Norway, Finland or even in parts of Asia.

- The more you invest in residential property, the more critical it becomes to understand the property cycle.

- The property cycle plays a critical role in any strategy to create wealth through property investment.

- Wise investors often hear the catch-cry 'But this time it's different because . . .' to justify why a current boom should last longer than ever before. But they understand that the basic principles of the property cycle remain the same, and many have used this knowledge to increase their financial net worth while minimising their investment risks.

- No doubt each new property cycle will bring new lessons, but the same pattern will be repeated again and again because it is subject to a combination of key drivers which affect supply and demand of property.

- Just like everything in life there are a few exceptions to the rules of the property cycle, but these do not represent the market as a whole.

- Sometimes specific, localised hot spots emerge regardless of a city's or region's property cycle. Eventually though, such hot spots will be subject to the property cycle because they will reach a level of relativity with surrounding or similar locations.

Chapter 2

Why the Property Cycle is Predictable

All cycles involve the repetition of specific periods of uniform activity. For example, no matter where you are in the world, every day is a cycle of twenty-four hours. Each day begins with the phase of morning; then the phase of afternoon begins; followed by the phase of night.

'The property cycle concept is simple to understand and the pattern it follows is predictable. Understanding the property cycle is as simple as understanding that night follows day.'

In the same way that a day always begins with morning, followed by afternoon and then night, the property cycle follows a uniform pattern: the recovery is followed by the boom, which is followed by the slump, which is followed by the beginning of the next property cycle with the recovery.

The progress of a day occurs naturally from the gravitational pull of the earth rotating around its axis creating the morning, afternoon and evening phases of each day. The property cycle also

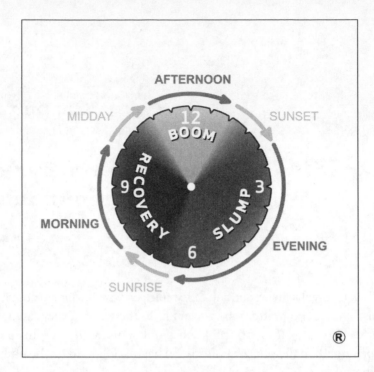

has its own gravitational pull created by the combined influence of several key drivers. These key drivers collectively build momentum which propels the property market through each of the three phases of the property cycle. Just like the irresistible force of gravity, these key drivers are the fundamental reason the property cycle moves through each of its phases.

Although every country in the world passes through a morning, afternoon and night every twenty-four hours, we know that seasonal influences result in longer or shorter days. Similarly, the length of each phase of the property cycle can also vary wildly as a result of local conditions – but the *pattern* remains the same.

The property cycle for specific cities can vary from that of the country as a whole as a result of the city's local key drivers. However, there is generally a close correlation between a city's property cycle and the country's cycle.

The property cycle for specific suburbs within cities can also vary from the city's overall cycle. Research undertaken in respect of

Valid photo ID required for all returns, exchanges and to receive and redeem store credit. With a receipt, a full refund in the original form of payment will be issued for new and unread books and unopened music within 14 days from any Barnes & Noble store. For merchandise purchased with a check, a store credit will be issued. **Without an original receipt**, a store credit issued by mail will be offered at the lowest selling price. With a receipt, returns of new and unread books and unopened music from bn.com can be made for store credit. A gift receipt or exchange receipt serves as proof of purchase price only. An exchange or store credit will be offered for new and unread books and unopened music/DVDs/audio for the price paid.

Valid photo ID required for all returns, exchanges and to receive and redeem store credit. With a receipt, a full refund in the original form of payment will be issued for new and unread books and unopened music within 14 days from any Barnes & Noble store. For merchandise purchased with a check, a store credit will be issued. **Without an original receipt**, a store credit issued by mail will be offered at the lowest selling price. With a receipt, returns of new and unread books and unopened music from bn.com can be made for store credit. A gift receipt or exchange receipt serves as proof of purchase price only. An exchange or store credit will be offered for new and unread books and unopened music/DVDs/audio for the price paid.

Valid photo ID required for all returns, exchanges and to receive and redeem store credit. With a receipt, a full refund in the original form of payment will be issued for new and unread books and unopened music within 14 days from any Barnes & Noble store. For merchandise purchased with a check, a store credit will be issued. **Without an original receipt**, a store credit issued by mail will be offered at the lowest selling price. With a receipt, suburbs or regions within a city indicates lower-priced suburbs, and the suburbs located furthest away from the CBD, are likely to be more cyclical than other suburbs within that city.[2] This appears to be caused by too many property investors buying property on the outskirts of cities, where typically higher returns can be achieved from rents compared with property prices. This becomes particularly evident at the end of the boom phase of the property cycle.

Introduction to the Key Drivers

The property cycle and the time on the property cycle clock are driven by a combination of key drivers. These include factors that influence supply and demand, such as *net migration, vacancy rates* and *property affordability*. The progression of the time on the property cycle clock is influenced primarily by changes in these key drivers. These changes are obviously beyond the control of individual property investors, just as the gravity that controls the progression of the phases of a day is beyond our control.

The length of a day varies from one season to another as a result of gravitational forces, and so too the length of each property cycle can vary depending on which key drivers are having the most influence and to what degree they are exerting their influence. The key drivers (outlined in detail in Chapter 5) reflect demographic, financial and emotional factors which all influence property supply and demand from different perspectives.

An example of a demographic key driver is population growth. Population growth traditionally peaks (i.e. is at a high) at the end of the boom phase of the property cycle and reaches a trough (i.e. is at a low) at the end of the slump phase.

By considering when the key drivers typically have reached a peak or a trough during former property cycles, we gain some insight into how to read future property cycles. Determining the property cycle phase at any given time involves a consideration of the activity of specific key drivers.

In Graph 2.1 on the next page, the thin line represents the annualised house price index percentage change (left-hand scale) and the thick line represents the annualised population percentage change (right-hand scale). The peak of population growth in New Zealand was reached at the end of the boom in 1996, and the trough was reached at the end of the slump in 2001.

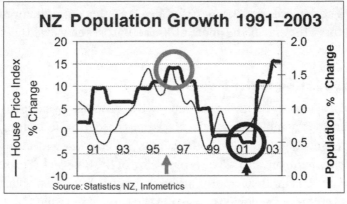

NZ Population Growth 1991–2003

Graph 2.1

Introduction to the Market Influencers

During my study of the factors impacting on the property market, I discovered that some, such as interest rates and inflation, are commonly thought to be key drivers of the property cycle. But when I considered these factors in the light of historical property cycles, I found they do not actually propel the property cycle through its phases. Instead, they simply have a short-term influence on the market that can cloud perception of what is happening to the property cycle. I call these factors *market influencers* because they influence the perceived duration of a specific phase of the property cycle.

Consider again the example of a day. If it is the afternoon and there is a sudden storm and clouds block the sun, then the day may appear to be moving into the night phase, even though it is still only the afternoon. I have found that market influencers can also be misleading. Many property investors gauge what is happening in the property market from the news media, which we all know survives and thrives on sensationalism. Unfortunately for these investors, media headlines do not always accurately represent the actual state of the property market. Media headlines can sometimes obscure what is actually happening during a phase of the property cycle and make it look as though the property market is moving into a different phase. For example, a significant terrorist attack (such as September 11, 2001) which affects confidence can almost stop the property market in its tracks for several weeks, maybe even for months. This may cause media commentators to believe the property market has slumped, when in fact this event is similar to a passing cloud that has temporarily cast a shadow over the day. Ironically, after the initial shock of such events has worn off, property investment can become vigorous as people seek the security of bricks and mortar as a 'safe' investment vehicle.

Market influencers often do become headline news, and cloud investors' judgement of what is really happening in the property cycle. Interest rates are a good example of a market influencer that is often confused as a key driver. For example if the property market is booming and interest rates increase significantly over a short time-frame, many property investors will perceive that the boom is over because of the higher interest rates making property investment less attractive. However, increased interest rates have historically had little influence on house prices.

Graph 2.2 below shows how, from 1984 to 1987, interest rates increased significantly, yet house prices surged upwards resulting in

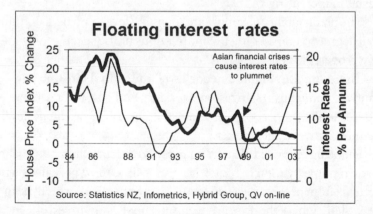

Graph 2.2

a boom. Then in 1988–91, interest rates decreased with no resultant surge in house price growth. If interest rates are a key driver of the property cycle then surely we should have witnessed the opposite effects during these periods (i.e. house price decreases in 1984–87 and house price increases in 1988–91).

We didn't see the effects we might have expected because a market influencer such as interest rates has the same effect on the property market as clouds blocking the sun during the cycle of a day. Interest rates will *not* drive the property cycle from one phase into the next, but they will often give the perception of doing so.

A classic example of this was the significant interest rate drop seen in 1998 (caused by the Asian financial crises) which led property investors to perceive that a boom was coming and resulted in a short-term house price surge in 1999. Many property investors interpreted the drop in interest rates as being adequate to create a property boom, but in fact it wasn't, as evidenced by house price erosion in 2000–01.

The Predictability of the Property Market Players

Like any commodity, property is influenced by supply and demand. An oversupply of property with inadequate demand will result in reducing values, just as high demand with inadequate supply will result in increasing values.

The predictability of supply and demand levels can be ascertained to a degree by considering the motivations of the specific 'players' in the property market.

There are four main categories of individuals in the property market: home buyers, investors, vendors and developers. There are phases in the property cycle when each one of these categories will be most active in the market.

Home buyers will typically be most prevalent when it is cheaper to own property than to rent. Investors will be most prevalent when returns from property exceed ownership costs. Vendors will be most prevalent when there are few home buyers or investors in the market, which is typically in the slump phase. Developers will be most prevalent when levels of high demand exist or there is a shortage of property for sale.

Home buyers are motivated primarily by a combination of emotional and financial considerations. For home buyers, financial considerations are often secondary to emotional considerations because lifestyle sacrifices will typically be made to enable an emotionally attractive property to be purchased.

Unlike home buyers, *investors* are motivated primarily by financial considerations and to a lesser degree by emotional considerations. However there are times in the property cycle when many investors succumb to the emotions of fear and greed (more about that in Chapter 4), rather than focusing on financial considerations. Investors can create significant demand and ongoing momentum in the property market. Often these investors already have a good level of financial resource in the form of equity in existing property and/or good cashflow to enable them to borrow to buy more property. Therefore they are often not limited to buying just one investment property.

Vendors who are also mostly home buyers (they are selling an existing home and buying a replacement home) are motivated by a combination of emotional and financial considerations. However, vendors who are investors cashing up property are motivated primarily by financial considerations. This is because their motivation to release cash by selling is greater than their emotional attachment to keep the property, otherwise they would not be in the market to sell!

Developers are motivated simply by profit. When demand is strong, developers will rapidly increase the volume of properties they are constructing and will maximise their profits by pricing property to ensure a quick turnover. But as demand reduces when the market inevitably suffers from an oversupply of properties, they will sacrifice profit margins to sell unsold stock. If they cannot secure sales, their financier may well enforce such sales to recoup the funds lent to the developer to build the unsold properties.

CHAPTER SUMMARY

- A property cycle is the repetition of specific periods of uniform activity.

- The property cycle concept is simple to understand and the pattern it follows is predictable. To understand the property cycle in its entirety is as simple as understanding that night follows day.

- Media headlines can sometimes cloud what is actually happening during a phase of the property cycle and make it look like the property market is moving into a different phase.

- There are four main categories of individuals in the property market at any given time. They are *home buyers*, *investors*, *vendors* and *developers*. There are phases in the property cycle when each one of these categories will be most active in the market.

Chapter 3

The Property Cycle Clock

The property cycle can be shown to follow a consistent pattern. To help gauge the progress of the property cycle I have invented the property cycle clock – a simple device that property investors can use to follow the progress of the property cycle.

Each phase of the property cycle is reflected by the state of the property market at that time. For example, in the boom phase property is an extremely popular investment vehicle and highly sought after. The property market is in a state of euphoria, as property investors and homeowners experience strong growth in the value of their property. However in the slump, and for some of the recovery phase, property is typically out of favour and therefore the state of the property market is somewhat subdued. Property is not experiencing strong growth in value and might even be experiencing a decline.

> 'The easiest way to understand the progress of the property cycle is to represent its phases by the circular shape of a typical clock.'

The illustration overleaf shows the three property cycle phases in the format of a clock face. This property cycle clock follows a

THE PROPERTY CYCLE CLOCK ®

clockwise movement from one phase into the next. However, unlike a normal clock, the length of each phase can vary from one property cycle to the next. Equally, the duration of one phase will not necessarily determine the duration of the following phases.

The concept of a clock has been adopted to enable us to estimate where the property market is in relation to the phases of the property cycle.

There are specific clues in the property market that clearly indicate which phase the property cycle is in. These include the key drivers (outlined in Chapter 5) as well as the manifestations of fear and greed (outlined in Chapter 4) seen in the attitudes of the general public. These manifestations often surface in media headlines as well as in casual discussions over a coffee with workmates, and often dominate discussions at dinner parties with friends and extended family members.

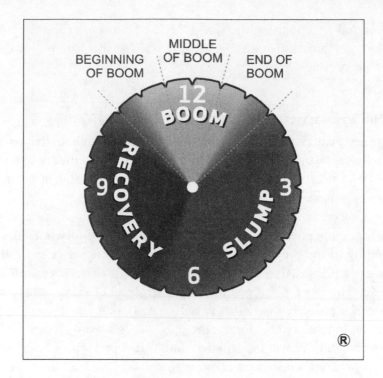

The Stages of Each Phase in the Property Cycle

Within each of the three phases of the property cycle there are three distinct stages. These stages simply signal the beginning of a phase, the middle and the end of each stage, as shown above.

Just as evidence exists in the form of clues to indicate which *phase* the property cycle is in, evidence also exists to indicate the specific *stage* of each phase at any given time. In Chapters 7–9 you will learn how to identify the approximate time of the property cycle clock in your locality, based on the key drivers influencing your local property market. You will also learn to identify the relevant manifestations of fear and greed that become evident at specific stages of each phase, the typical media headlines you can expect to see at each stage, and their influence on the property cycle in your city, region or district.

For many years there have been various forms of economic clocks used to outline economic changes typically experienced by mature economies throughout the world. My trademarked property cycle clock similarly offers an insight into the specific progress of the property cycle.

The Property Cycle Clock and Property Values

Property values are measured in various ways throughout the world including by averages, medians and varying forms of indexes. Some of these measurements produce an inaccurate indication of what is actually happening to property values.

It surprises me how often less reliable data, such as average or median sale prices, are quoted as a representation of what's happening in the property market, because these figures can easily present a distorted view. This can arise in several ways. For example: when there is a disproportionately high level of sales activity of superior property in an area in a given period, it may appear that values in that area are increasing purely because the average and/ or median price will look higher than it had previously. Prices for such superior property may have actually *decreased* but this may not be borne out by the average or median figures. Conversely, such a period may be followed by a high level of sales activity of inferior property in the same area, which may seem to indicate that values in the area are decreasing purely because the average and median sale prices will be lower. The fact may be that there were few sales of superior property, so while average and median figures indicate that values are declining, they may actually be increasing.

So be careful when considering which property price measurement tool to follow, as some of them can give you a completely wrong indication of what is happening to property values.

> 'The most accurate measures of property values I have found are commonly referred to as 'house price indexes'. These, instead of measuring the sale price of property in isolation, are benchmarked to some alternative but appropriate measure.'

A good example of this is the house price index used in New Zealand and produced by the local state-owned enterprise Quotable Value Ltd. This index measures residential property value growth based on actual sales data benchmarked as a percentage of the rateable value (formerly known as Government Valuation or GV). This house price index is considered by many economists to be the most accurate house price trend indicator available in New Zealand.

There are specific effects on the property market which occur at certain times on the property cycle clock. These effects include the general rise and fall of property values and rents as set out below:

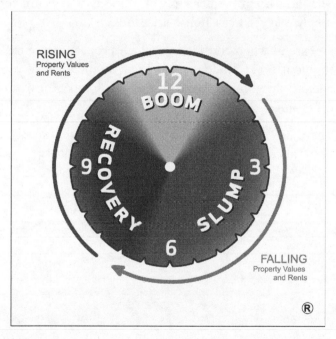

While the above illustration indicates the general direction of property values and rents, this does not mean that values cannot rise when the property market is in a slump or cannot fall when the property market is in a boom. There will always be exceptions, but the trends of property values and rents do tend to be consistent with this illustration. Property cannot experience consistent value increases throughout a slump, just as it cannot experience consistent value decreases in a boom.

CHAPTER SUMMARY

- The property cycle clock is a simple device that property investors can use to follow the progress of the property cycle.

- Within each of the three phases of the property cycle there are three distinct stages. These stages are the *beginning*, *middle* and *end* of each phase of the property cycle.

- The most accurate measures of property values are commonly referred to as 'house price indexes'.

- Be careful when considering which property price measurement tool to follow as some of them can give you a completely wrong perception of what is happening to property values.

- There are specific effects on the property market which occur at certain times on the property cycle clock.

Chapter 4

Fear and Greed in the Property Cycle

The property cycle acts as a catalyst for the powerful emotions of fear and greed in the general public. These emotions are provoked by various concerns and manifest in different forms throughout the property cycle. They are also very predictable according to which phase the property cycle is in.

> 'If the acronym for FEAR is *False Evidence Appearing Real* then the acronym for GREED may well be *Great Ridiculous Expectations Ending Disastrously!*'

One should not underestimate the rapid effect these powerful emotions can have on the majority of investors. The same emotions have resulted in huge losses being experienced not only in property markets but also in just about every other investment vehicle. Just think back to the 1987 sharemarket crash or the more recent dot.com crash.

Ironically, many of the fears experienced by investors throughout the property cycle will eventuate as a result of those fears, just as many investors motivated by greed will suffer the consequences of such greed.

The Motivators of Fear and Greed in the Property Cycle

The factors that generate fear and greed throughout the property cycle are intriguing and closely linked.

The various forms of fear experienced cause property investors either to take action, avoid action or simply do nothing. These fears are often not consciously considered to be the reasons for specific action or inaction, but operate in the subconscious mind as prime motivators. It is well known that we will do more to avoid pain than we will to pursue pleasure, therefore it is no surprise that fear is the major motivating emotion through most of the property cycle.

Common motivators of fear during the property cycle are:

● The potential for a repeat of history, resulting in loss.

● The potential to fail by missing out, resulting in loss of opportunity.

● Potential egotistical risk resulting in embarrassment.

● Potential financial risk resulting in financial burden.

The motivators of greed are similar to those of fear but are accompanied by an opposite expectation. While greed is a strong motivator, it is easy to see why it does not have the same power as fear when you understand that the potential gains can be far outweighed by the potential losses (which motivate fear).

Common motivators of greed during the property cycle are:

● The potential for a repeat of recent history, resulting in a profit.

● The potential for success by capitalising on opportunity.

● Potential egotistical boost resulting in pride.

● Potential financial reward resulting in fast wealth.

The Manifestations of Fear and Greed in the Property Cycle

Fear and greed manifest themselves in various forms throughout the property cycle. If we consider *how* these motivators actually work, we gain some insight into why people react in the way that they do throughout the property cycle.

Manifestations of Fear

1. *The potential for a repeat of history, resulting in loss.* The fear that history will repeat itself is usually experienced by investors who have formerly suffered either financially or emotionally (or both) as a result of a previous investment undertaking. This fear can cause different responses in property investors. It can stop an investor from buying any more property and/or it can inspire them to sell property investments they already own.

   Many investors without much property investment experience this fear, and sell their investments at the wrong time in the property cycle.

   An example of this is an investor I spoke with recently who had bought a property in 1997 near the peak of the last boom for $120,000; three years later in 2000 it was worth only $80,000 as a result of a slump in property values. He told me he then sold it in the 2002 recovery because he could get $91,000 for it and feared that he would suffer a greater loss if history repeated itself and values decreased again. He lost nearly $30,000!

2. *The potential to fail by missing out, resulting in loss of opportunity.* The fear of missing out is often experienced by investors who have previously missed out. The classic case of this fear resulting in a less than desirable situation is the investor who first procrastinates while waiting for property to prove itself as a wise investment.

In the meantime they pass up many opportunities . The property cycle moves through the recovery and then enters the boom phase before this investor finally decides that they have been missing out, and their fear of continuing to miss out becomes the major motivator that spurs them into action. Now they have a need to buy a property to overcome this fear. Unfortunately, there is a good chance this fear will emerge at the height of the boom phase of the property cycle.

3. *Potential egotistical risk resulting in embarrassment.* The fear of failure can paralyse investors, stopping them from making any decision at all. This fear is often apparent in investors who have suffered embarrassement in the past from another investment failure. It is commonly exhibited as 'paralysis by analysis', resulting in no action at all. The theory is, that at least then you can't be wrong because you never made a decision anyway.

An example of this was a new client of my firm who several years earlier had made some property investment decisions. His wife had questioned his judgement at the time. Years later the decisions proved to be bad ones resulting in real financial loss. He was embarrassed as a result. This time round he was wiser as he was seeking a professional opinion on an opportunity to buy a property. When I saw the details of the property he had considered buying, I told him to buy it immediately because it was a great opportunity compared to others I had recently seen. But he had already spent a week considering whether or not it was a good opportunity. He told me the property agent had called him that morning to tell him it was sold. When I asked him why he spent so long considering whether or not he should buy it, he said that he thought it was too good to be true so something must be wrong with it. He was so convinced something was amiss that he had analysed it from every angle for the past week – but still he couldn't find anything wrong with it. His fear of making a mistake, and subsequently feeling embarrassed, had been his downfall as he missed out on a fantastic opportunity.

Ironically, his fear of making a mistake and feeling embarrassed led him to spend too long analysing the investment which meant he missed out on what really was a superb opportunity.

He should have made an offer for the property subject to an acceptable term of due diligence, so he could still check the opportunity properly before deciding on whether or not to proceed. It amazes me how often I hear similar stories from property investors who just let a superb opportunity go by. The fear of failure is very common.

4. *Potential financial risk resulting in financial burden.* The fear of financial risk is often experienced by those who have formerly been risk-averse. Typically these investors will have worked hard to accumulate the wealth they already have and appreciate how long it can take to create wealth. They will procrastinate on property opportunities to avoid potential financial risk and sometimes also suffer from the fear of missing out (see point 2 above).

Manifestations of Greed

1. *The potential for a repeat of recent history, resulting in a profit.* Typically this form of greed is apparent in those who have not experienced earlier cycles in the property market. These investors fully expect property prices to continue to boom just because they have in the recent past. Often they will expect the first boom they experience to produce ever-increasing property values regardless of the key drivers of the property cycle.

2. *The potential for success by capitalising on opportunity.* This form of greed manifests in the belief that the more property you can accumulate, the better off you will be. It ignores the fact

that greater exposure to property does not guarantee your success as a property investor. Those suffering from this form of greed will consistently extend their financial resources to accumulate property, and eventually will regret this attitude when the slump phase erodes their financial position.

The best example I can give of this is my own circumstances in the late 1980s when I had a large exposure to property up to the limit of my financial resources. I was heavily committed financially, and at one stage was waiting for my next payday before I could pay my credit card bill. I was working full-time and also had part-time employment as a gas attendant to make ends meet. And then I got a phone call from my credit card company. The guy on the phone told me I was a week late paying my $50 credit card bill and he wanted to know when I would be paying it. I explained to him that I had very limited funds and the only money I had left was already reserved for food shopping. He said he didn't care what the money was reserved for, because I had to pay the credit card bill or else the credit card company would place a default notice against my credit record. So I had a choice: I could either pay the credit card bill and keep a clean credit rating but go hungry, or I could buy food for the next week and the credit card company would ruin my clean credit rating. I knew the consequence of not having a clean credit rating was very bad because it meant my ability to borrow might be adversely affected, but I had only a small amount of rice and a few cans of food left in the pantry and not much else to eat. So what did I do? The answer was simple. I was committed to keeping a clean credit rating because I knew how critical it was to my ability to borrow in the future for further property investments so I told him I would pay them their $50 the next day . . . and I did! My greed to increase my returns by maximising my exposure to property meant that I went hungry for a few days, but at least my credit rating remained intact.

Succumbing to this manifestation of greed can have severe consequences, and potentially the financial burden can be too high to bear. I learned a hard lesson.

3. *Potential egotistical boost resulting in pride.* Many investors will share the experiences of their newfound success with their family and friends. To be admired by those closest to you is certainly a source of pride. Unfortunately some investors feel the need to prove themselves to be ever more successful with their investment successes and this can result in over-extending their financial position.

4. *Potential financial reward resulting in fast wealth.* This manifests itself in the form of speculation. Such speculation is usually most evident at the end of a boom when many short-term investors buy property and then on-sell it for a quick profit. Usually there is little discretion applied to such purchases, as a common belief is that it doesn't matter what property you buy – if you just tidy it up you can on-sell it easily for a substantial profit.

The Prevalence of Fear and Greed

Fear and greed are common among the general public depending on the stage of the property cycle. The levels vary through the phases of the cycle from very high to almost non-existent.

Greed is the prevalent motivating emotion at the height of the boom until well into the slump when property value growth has softened. Greed, though, is overtaken by fear and almost disappears near the end of the slump when the property market bottoms out.

Fear is prevalent from early in the slump phase and increases in intensity as property values decline throughout the slump. In a typical property cycle this fear will stop most property investors from purchasing more property, and will last for several years until the property cycle moves into its next boom phase. The level of fear among most property investors will then decrease to its lowest levels

at the height of the boom as former anxieties do not materialise and memories of the slump fade.

Surprisingly the lessons of risk are not quickly learned by many property investors; this may be a result of the property cycle's longevity, spanning many years. It seems that levels of fear in the property cycle take a long time to subside but levels of greed rise quickly.

CHAPTER SUMMARY

- The property cycle acts as a catalyst for the powerful emotions of fear and greed in the general public.

- The various forms of fear experienced throughout the property cycle cause property investors either to take action, avoid action or simply do nothing. These fears are often not consciously acknowledged as the reasons for specific action or inaction, but operate in the subconscious mind as prime motivators.

- The various motivators of greed are similar to those of fear but are accompanied by an opposite expectation.

- The motivating factors of both fear and greed manifest themselves in various forms throughout the property cycle.

- Greed is prevalent from the middle of the boom until well into the slump.

- Fear is prevalent from early in the slump phase and increases in intensity as property values decline throughout the slump.

- Surprisingly, the lessons of risk are not quickly learned by many property investors; this may be a result of the property cycle's longevity, spanning many years.

Chapter 5

Key Drivers of the Property Cycle

Key drivers propel the property market through the various phases of the property cycle. Some of these key drivers are volatile and as a result can rapidly drive the property cycle through its phases, but others are more stable and take much longer to change.

> 'It is the *combined effect* of various key driver activities that can quickly thrust the property cycle through one phase and into the next, and no single key driver can propel the property cycle through a complete phase.'

It is important to understand that these key drivers propel the property cycle *collectively* rather than individually. Key drivers operate like a combination lock. Rather than having a single key to unlock the door to the next phase, the correct combination of several drivers is needed. Having one or two parts of the combination will not unlock the door. Similarly, the movement of one or two key drivers alone has little impact on the property cycle.

Some of the key drivers result from demographic changes such as population growth which can quickly increase demand for

GROW RICH with the PROPERTY CYCLE

property. Other key drivers are the result of financial changes such as an increase in the level of rents, which impacts on the financial viability of property investment. Yet other key drivers are influenced by emotions such as the number of days it takes to sell property and can induce panic buying, driven by a fear of missing out on the wave of capital growth, seen during the boom phase of the property cycle.

I have divided these key drivers into three categories: *demographic, financial* and *emotional.*

The Categories of Key Drivers

Demographic

Demographic key drivers determine the level of physical demand for property. They include such things as *population levels, net migration, employment levels,* the *number of people per household, vacancy rates of rental property* and the *scale of property construction.*

Financial

Financial key drivers relate to the financial viability of property, either as an investment vehicle or for owner occupation. They include *rental levels, return on investment, income levels, rental affordability, property affordability, finance availability* and *property values.*

Emotional

Emotional key drivers impact on confidence in property as a sound investment, and they have a powerful influence on the psychological reasons people buy property. They include the *average number of days it takes to sell property,* the *number of listings of property for sale, sales levels* and *gentrification* (upgrading of amenities, facilities and/or property).

These three categories of key drivers collectively create a momentum that impacts on the progression of the property cycle through each phase and from one phase into the next.

Key Driver Patterns

Each key driver follows a similar pattern. For example, return on investment will increase over time, reaching a peak (just before it is about to start declining); then returns will decrease until they bottom out (just before they are about to start increasing again).

This pattern can be compared to the cycle of a twenty-four hour day. In other words, the key drivers will follow the pattern below:

Increasing	=	Sunrise
Peak	=	Midday
Decreasing	=	Sunset
Trough	=	Midnight

So let's consider the pattern of one of the key drivers, return on investment:

Return on investment:

Direction	Property Cycle Phase
Increasing	End of Slump to Mid-Recovery
Peak	Mid-Recovery
Decreasing	End of Recovery to Mid-Slump
Trough	Mid-Slump to End-Slump

My research has shown that when we consider each of the key drivers in light of the property cycle, we find that the key driver patterns typically occur within specific phases of the property cycle. This helps us to identify which part of the property cycle the property market is experiencing at any given time.

By understanding the key drivers' patterns you can use the property cycle to your advantage by knowing what to expect property values to do in the short to medium term.

Below are graphs for many of the key drivers in New Zealand since 1990. I have highlighted when each key driver experiences a peak and trough on each graph.

I have also outlined which key drivers experience peaks or troughs during each of the three phases of the property cycle: recovery, boom and slump (Chapters 7–9).

Key Driver Factors

The main factors that operate within each key driver are given below:

Note: in the key driver graphs the thin line represents the annualised house price index percentage change (left-hand scale) and the thick line represents the annualised percentage change in the key driver (right-hand scale). Each peak is highlighted with a grey circle and a grey arrow points to the year in which the peak occurred. Each trough is highlighted with a black circle and a black arrow points to the year in which the trough occurred.

DEMOGRAPHICS

Net Migration or Population Change
(Immigrants plus number of births) less (emigrants plus number of deaths). This results either in an increasing or a decreasing population.

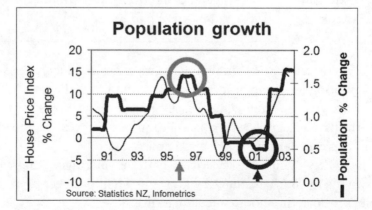

Graph 5.1

Population changes can often be rapid, causing a sudden surge or drop in demand.

A sudden increase in population can result in strong growth in rental levels as additional properties cannot easily be supplied quickly. Population growth peaks at the end of the boom and troughs at the end of the slump.

Property Construction

The amount of new properties being constructed.

Construction tends to lag behind any increased demand for properties due to the significant lead time required to build. This lag can and usually does result in an eventual oversupply of property, long after the actual demand for additional properties has dissipated. Construction levels peak at the end of the boom and trough mid- to end of the slump.

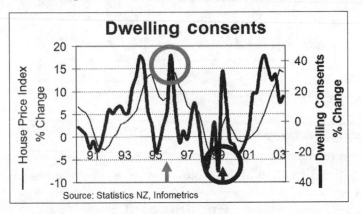

Graph 5.2

Property Vacancy Rates

The number of vacant properties available to rent divided by the total number of properties available to rent.

Vacancy rates will trough during the recovery phase and peak during the slump.

(Data not available for New Zealand vacancy rates.)

Number of People per Household

Total population divided by total number of properties.

The number of people per household will increase once rents reach unaffordable levels and when rents become very affordable (usually as a result of increased vacancy rates) the number of people per household will decrease. The number of people per household will peak near the beginning of the slump and trough near the end of the slump.

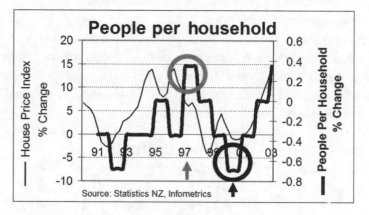

Graph 5.3

Employment Levels

The percentage of employable people actually in employment.

When there are high employment levels there is usually an

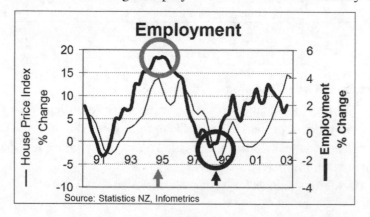

Graph 5.4

upward pressure on incomes which assists with the affordability of property and rents. Conversely, low employment levels will result in static incomes and therefore property and rents become less affordable. Employment levels will peak in the mid- to end of the boom and trough in the mid- to end of the slump.

FINANCIAL

Gross Return on Investment (ROI)

Gross annual rental income (based on market rates) divided by the market value of the property.

Investment funds are fickle when it comes to the direction in which they flow, and investment opportunities other than property will continually be compared to returns being achieved on property. Investment funds often flow towards the highest available returns from the choices of property, shares, bonds and bank deposits. The ROI of property peaks during the recovery phase and will trough during the early stages of the slump.

(Inadequate data available for New Zealand.)

Average Rents

Average levels of rent payable.

Rental levels typically overcompensate for increased demand during the boom and reach unsustainably high levels. They then undercompensate for decreased demand during the slump and reach

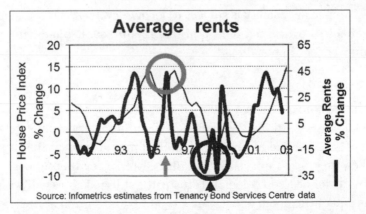

Graph 5.5

very low levels. Rents will peak near the middle of the boom and trough near the middle of the slump.

Average Incomes

Average incomes before tax.

Incomes assist with the affordability of rental levels and property ownership. Income growth will peak near the end of the boom and trough near the end of the slump.

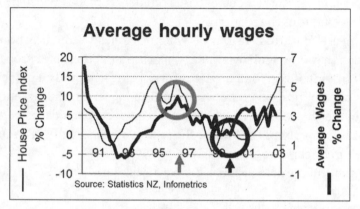

Graph 5.6

Finance Availability

Availability of financing for property purchases.

Finance availability is subject to its own cycle. It is more readily available during the boom and less readily available during the slump (refer Chapter 12).

Property Values

Market value based on a willing buyer/willing seller.

Like rents, property values typically overcompensate for increased demand at the end of the boom and early in the slump, when they reach unsustainably high levels. They then undercompensate for decreased demand during the slump. Values will peak at the end of the boom or early in the slump and trough at the end of the slump.

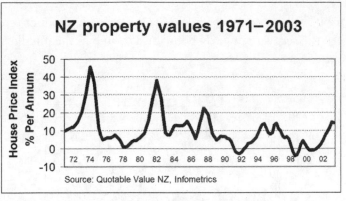

Graph 5.7

Property Affordability

Measure of how affordable it is to own or invest in property.

Affordability is affected by several factors including finance availability, interest rates, income levels and rental levels which all affect borrowers' borrowing capacity. Property becomes least affordable during the beginning of the slump and most affordable during the recovery.

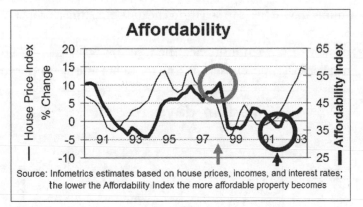

Graph 5.8

Gross Domestic Product

Gross Domestic Product (GDP) is a measure of a country's output and is based on the market value of goods and services produced.

Property and associated products and services make a significant contribution to a country's GDP. Gross Domestic Product tends to peak in the recovery or early boom and trough in the middle of the slump.

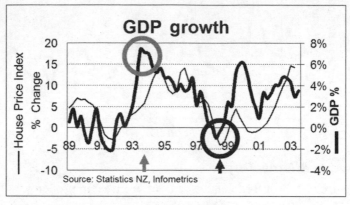

Graph 5.9

EMOTIONAL

Number of Days it Takes to Sell Property

How many days it takes to sell from the date of listing a property for sale.

This key driver can influence the levels of fear experienced by potential property purchasers during the boom and by vendors dur-

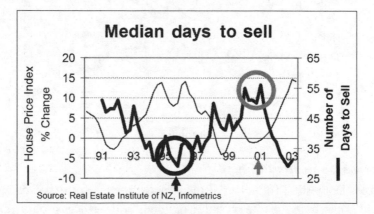

Graph 5.10

ing the slump. For example, during the boom potential purchasers fear that if they do not make a rapid decision, they may miss out on the wave of capital growth in values as properties are selling rapidly. During the slump vendors fear that if they do not place a realistic price on their property it may take a long time to secure a sale. The number of days to sell peaks at the end of the slump and troughs at the mid- to end of the boom.

Gentrification

Upgrade of properties, amenities or services in a specific location.

Gentrification is prolific at the end of the boom when many people utilise their increased equity (as a result of the boom) to finance the refurbishment of property in an attempt to further increase its value or rental income. Gentrification can create powerful emotions in purchasers and motivate them to pay a premium for properties which are upgraded to a superior standard. Gentrification peaks at the end of the boom and troughs at the beginning of the recovery.

(Data not available for New Zealand.)

Property Listings

The number of properties available for sale (or listed for sale with real estate agents).

Property listings will peak in comparison to sales volumes during the slump phase as the supply of property exceeds demand, and then reach a trough during the boom when properties are selling rapidly. This key driver, like the number of days it takes to sell property, can also cause potential property purchasers to fear they may miss out on the wave of capital growth during the boom phase of the property cycle. During the slump, vendors fear that if they do not place a realistic price on their property it may take a long time to sell due to the high number of property listings during this phase.

Vendors are only too aware of how to make their property more noticeable to the few purchasers in the market during the slump – and that is to discount their selling price significantly.

(Data not available for New Zealand.)

Property Sales Volumes

The number of property sales.

Sales volumes will peak near the end of the boom phase and trough near the end of the slump. During the boom, inexperienced investors become aware of the high level of sales and fear they may be missing out because so many other investors are buying so much property! During the slump many investors are fearful of the low level of sales, as they realise that property is no longer an asset that can be quickly realised if they need to sell.

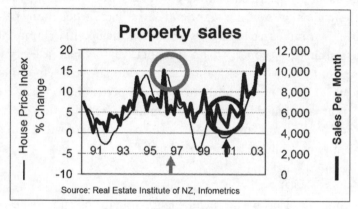

Graph 5.11

CHAPTER SUMMARY

- Key drivers propel the property market through the various phases of the property cycle.

- It is important to understand that these key drivers propel the property cycle *collectively* rather than individually.

- There are three major categories of key drivers: *demographic, financial* and *emotional*.

- Demographic key drivers determine the level of demand for property.

- Financial key drivers relate to the financial viability of property either as an investment or for owner occupation.

- Emotional key drivers impact on confidence in property as a sound investment, and have a powerful influence on the psychological reasons people buy property.

- The key drivers follow a similar pattern, peaking and reaching a trough at specific phases of the property cycle.

- By understanding the key drivers' patterns, you can use the property cycle to your advantage by knowing what to expect property values to do in the short to medium term.

Chapter 6

Market Influencers of the Property Cycle

Market influencers are factors that affect the perception of the length of a specific phase of the property cycle. It is important to understand that these market influencers are often confused with key drivers of the property cycle.

> 'In contrast to key drivers, which actually propel the property cycle from one phase into the next, market influencers impact on the immediate levels of supply and demand in the property market – but their impact is temporary.'

Market influencers have little to do with the fundamental key drivers of the property cycle.

As explained in Chapter 2, market influencers have the same effect on the property market as clouds blocking the sun during the cycle of a day, and can easily give a false impression. They will not drive the property cycle from one phase into the next. However they will often give the *perception* that is what is happening. The great news about market influencers is that they can create a window of opportunity for prudent investors. These opportunities arise as a direct result of the confusion created by the market influencers in terms of what is really happening in the market.

Even though the presence of dark clouds does not indicate that it is night time, they can create that impression. For example, clouds can sometimes appear during an afternoon and give the perception that night is arriving. But an hour or two later the clouds might dissipate, revealing that it is still actually only afternoon. So too can market influencers temporarily influence the property market either positively or negatively, irrespective of which phase it is in. It is because market influencers can temporarily affect the property market that they are often confused with key drivers.

This is exactly what was experienced late in 1994 in New Zealand during the middle of the 1994 to 1996 boom. At that time the market influencer, mortgage interest rates, lifted to 11% per annum. Many investors assumed the boom was therefore at an end and stopped buying. This created a sudden surplus of keen vendors unable to find buyers for their properties. At that time I recognised that the boom was not in fact over, but had simply stalled, because I understood that interest rates were not the only determining factor of property values.

It was at this time that I purchased a house in an Auckland suburb for just $155,000, even though it was valued at over $170,000. The vendors had committed to buying another house and no one else had made an offer to buy their existing house. Then interest rates reduced and the stalled boom resumed its progress: I sold the same house (due to a change in my own circumstances) within eight months for $188,000.

While market influencers affect our perceptions, we should also be aware that perception sometimes can become reality. Market influencers can occasionally influence the property cycle's key drivers, and therefore indirectly influence the progress of the property cycle. For example, if a key influencer like interest rates increased and remained high. This would ultimately reduce property affordability, which is a key driver of the property cycle. But bear in mind it takes a *combination* of key drivers to propel the property cycle.

Market influencers can affect the property market at any phase of the property cycle and are not typically predictable in the same way as are key drivers. Market influences usually produce reactive decisions from most uninformed property investors, but offer a platform for savvy property investors to make proactive decisions. This is because savvy investors know how to recognise the difference between market influencers and key drivers, and use the market influencer's impact on the property market to their advantage.

> 'Market influencers are considered to be the wise property investor's friend, because they often present opportunities or indicate the need for extra caution which would otherwise never have arisen.'

The Classic Market Influencers

These are:

● Interest rates.

● Confidence in property as an investment vehicle.

● Inflation.

● Legislative amendments (taxation and/or local authority).

● Offshore investors in local property.

● Investment alternatives.

The Impacts of Market Influencers

The following impacts and perceptions are based on each market influencer acting in isolation. In the event that several market influencers are affecting the market at the same time, the impact on the market becomes much less predictable.

Impact of Interest Rates

Interest rates can (and do) move either up or down at any phase of the property cycle.

If interest rates increase during the boom phase of the property cycle there is every likelihood that the boom phase will appear to be nearing its end. Such an interest rate increase typically invokes a fear response from inexperienced property investors, who will be less inclined to seek purchases because of their perception that the boom may soon be over. This perception can in fact temporarily stall the progression of the cycle.

Experienced investors will be more interested in watching the key drivers, and if these indicate the boom still has some time to run they will be very active during this time, seeking to purchase property (especially from keen vendors concerned with the interest rate increase). These experienced investors understand that the boom does not end purely as a result of higher interest rates.

Alternatively, if interest rates *decrease* during the boom phase of the property cycle the common perception is that the boom will most likely last for quite some time. This typically invokes a greed response from inexperienced property investors, as they will recklessly buy more property at higher prices as a result of lower interest rates. In fact, it is likely that the progression of the cycle will gain momentum as a result.

Experienced investors will be watching the key drivers rather than purely interest rates – if these indicate the boom is nearly over, they will be reluctant to purchase more property during this time as they know a slump is coming which will be likely to deliver much better opportunities than those currently available.

Note in Graph 6.1 below that when interest rates decreased in the slump in 1998 as a result of the Asian financial crises, there was a surge in house prices shortly afterwards (during 1999). This surge was based largely on the perception that the property market would boom as a result of low interest rates. However, this was not a recovery of the property market based on the key drivers. The perception that the market would soon recover is why house price growth accelerated in 1999, but then it stalled and actually declined in 2000. The reduced interest rates did not drive the property cycle out of the slump and into the boom phase even though many investors perceived that was exactly what would occur. If interest rates were a key driver then we would see a much clearer correlation between interest rate levels and house price growth.

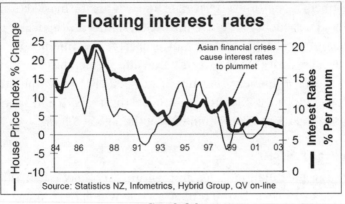

Graph 6.1

Impact of Confidence in Property as an Investment Vehicle

The effect of confidence in property as an investment vehicle builds momentum over time. Confidence tends to react to the state of the property market rather than having an impact on the property cycle. The longer confidence trends in a particular direction, the greater the degree of confidence will have on the perceived longevity of the property cycle.

For example, when confidence increases consistently, the property cycle will appear to accelerate irrespective of the phase of the property cycle. This is because confidence is a strong underlying psychological factor which influences people's willingness to make a large financial commitment (such as purchasing property). Equally, when confidence in property as an investment is consistently decreasing, the property cycle will appear to stall. This is because people's willingness to make a large financial commitment will diminish as confidence decreases.

Local confidence levels are often exaggerated or influenced by international confidence levels. A change in international confidence can often have a rapid effect on local confidence, because for international confidence to become headline news locally there is usually some drastic situation which either has occurred or is about to occur. The impact of such a change in international confidence can have varying effects on local confidence in property as an investment. For example, terrorism and war are the most likely international confidence negative influencers, and yet the likely result will be to increase confidence in property investment due to the perceived security of property, as seen after September 11.

Negative influencers are much more likely to become quickly evident, and have a resultant impact, than positive influencers, because bad news travels much faster than good news.

Impact of Inflation

The impact of inflation builds momentum over time. When inflation increases consistently, the property cycle will appear to accelerate irrespective of the phase of the property cycle. This is because inflation typically flows on to increased incomes, household and construction costs, and subsequent upward pressure on house prices. Temporary demand for property remains strong irrespective of the key drivers because property is considered to be an inflation-proof investment.

Note in Graph 6.2 that New Zealand's inflation peaks and troughs have no consistent correlation with house price movements. The

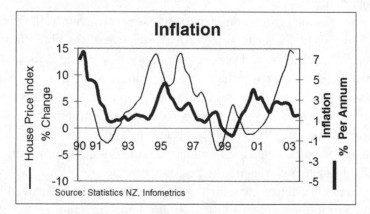

Graph 6.2

perceptions created by the market influencer of inflation have little to do with the key drivers that influence the property cycle. Therefore even when inflation is low we can still experience a property market recovery and boom, and even when inflation is high we can still experience a property market slump.

Impact of Legislative Amendments

Amendments to legislation can have a sudden effect on the market due to the instant (but short-lived) impact they can have on demand.

Impact of positive amendment

A positive legislative amendment relating to property ownership or investment will appear to extend the boom and recovery phases because it will encourage the purchase of property and increase demand. But it will appear to shorten the slump phase because the amended legislation will make it more attractive to buy property. It can appear that the slump is over, as demand suddenly increases.

Impact of negative amendment

A negative legislative amendment will have the opposite effect, as it becomes less attractive to buy property. Therefore it appears to herald the end of the boom and recovery phases. But it will appear to prolong the slump because property becomes even less attractive to invest in at a time when it is already out of favour.

Impacts of Offshore Investors in Local Property Market

An influx or exodus of offshore investors buying or selling property in the local market often has an immediate result. Offshore investors tend to follow a 'herd' mentality due to their distance from local knowledge of the market, so tend to have a sudden impact on the market. Offshore investors' decisions on where to invest can be fickle and can create volatility in the local market.

Impact of increased number of offshore investors

A strong increase in offshore investors can appear to prolong the boom phase, as there will be a larger pool of buyers fuelling the market. However it can appear to push the slump phase into the recovery phase due to the sudden increase in demand for property created by these offshore buyers.

Impact of decreased number of offshore investors
A large decrease in offshore investors investing in the local market during a boom can appear to herald the end of the boom, as less demand is apparent. Conversely, it can appear to prolong the slump phase as there will suddenly be a smaller pool of potential property buyers.

Impact of Alternative Investments
Alternative investment vehicles are always being compared to property investment. A significant number of investment funds will gravitate towards the most favourable investment vehicle of the time. The herd mentality tends to dominate the direction in which these investment funds flow. Remember when technology shares became the favoured investment at the end of the 1990s, attracting a huge flow of investment funds until their spectacular demise? At the time it would have been wise to invest in property instead, but investment funds chased the expected higher returns available from potential capital growth in technology shares.

Increased favour of investment alternatives
If alternative investments to property increase in favour during the boom phase, this phase can appear to be shortened as less demand exists for property. However if this increase in favour occurs during the slump, the slump phase can appear to be prolonged as house price growth decreases as a result of less demand.

Decreased favour of investment alternatives
If alternative investments decrease in favour then, irrespective of which phase the property cycle is in, the perception will always be that the current phase will be shortened. This is because in the absence of attractive alternatives, investment funds will flow into property and the increased demand will put upward pressure on house price growth, which in turn gives the appearance of accelerating the current phase.

Market Influencers Bring Opportunity

Market influencers often provide the kind of sensational headlines that newspapers thrive on.

It is critical that you watch for these influencers and be aware of their limited effect on the longevity of the specific phases of the property cycle.

You can act in a countercyclical way to the market by learning to recognise these market influencers. As a result you will be able to take advantage of any temporary drop in demand because of bad news which may actually result only in a short-term decrease in demand. Market influencers can sometimes be the clouds with a silver lining!

Conversely, the ability to recognise market influencers that will deliver a short-term increase in demand will allow you to become more circumspect in your investment activities. Being aware of market influencers and their effect on the property cycle provides informed property investors with a greater degree of foresight than most other investors. This in turn allows you to become proactive rather than reactive with your investment activities.

CHAPTER SUMMARY

- Market influencers are factors that affect the general public's perception of the length of a specific phase of the property cycle.

- Market influencers often cloud property investors' judgement as to what is really happening in the property cycle.

- Market influencers typically produce reactive decisions from most uninformed property investors, but offer a platform for savvy property investors to make proactive decisions.

- It is important to differentiate between key drivers of the property cycle and market influencers, because you can then act in a countercyclical way to the market.

- Market influencers are considered to be the wise property investor's friends because they often present opportunities or warn of the need for extra caution which would never have arisen otherwise.

- You can act in a countercyclical way to the market by learning to recognise these market influencers. This means that you may be able to take advantage of any temporary drop in demand because of bad news which will result in only a short-term decrease in demand.

PART 2

The Phases of the Property Cycle

Chapter 7

The Recovery Phase

The recovery is an exciting phase of the property cycle. It offers a wealth of opportunity but is not easily recognised by most investors.

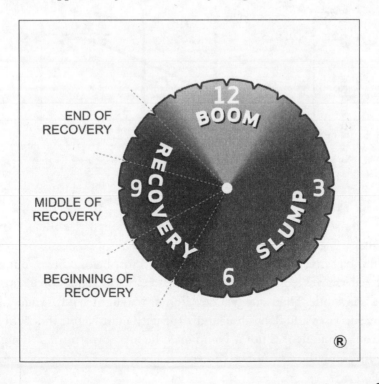

Property values rise relatively sharply during the recovery. There are bargains everywhere, but many people hesitate because they are unsure of whether the increased demand for property is actually a recovery of the property market which will lead to a boom or merely a short-term lift in demand which will soon subside. Some of those who *do* recognise the recovery has commenced incorrectly perceive that values are booming instead of actually recovering, and mistakenly interpret this phase as being a boom.

> 'Many property market observers mistakenly believe that a property boom has begun when the property cycle enters the beginning of the recovery phase.'

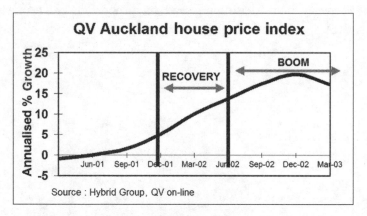

Graph 7.1

The recovery phase can be likened to the sunrise. Before the sunrise everything is dark as the previous night comes to a close. They say that the night is always darkest just before dawn, but as the sun moves closer to breaching the horizon the reduction in darkness is subtle. Then slowly it gets lighter and lighter until suddenly the sun rises and floods the landscape with light. While this light is strong, initially it is not accompanied by much warmth, although before long the warmth increases.

So too the recovery phase seems to be subtle in its arrival, until suddenly property values start to rise and everyone recognises the recovery. But many wonder where the increasing warmth of sustained price growth is. This warmth arrives only when the recovery has well and truly taken hold.

The Beginning of the Recovery

At this point two key drivers – population and rental costs – start to rise rapidly, almost taking the market by surprise. Suddenly it seems there is a shortage of available property to rent compared with the many people who seem to be in the market. There is also an increase in existing property owners' equity levels, as property values start to rise at single digit levels (under 10%) on an annualised basis. An increasing return on investment is noticeable as rent increases initially outpace increasing property values. Affordability levels are high at this point of the property cycle. Property finance becomes easier to qualify for, and the ability to purchase property with a relatively low cash input becomes a reality. It seems the ability to purchase a property is within reach for many people at this time.

Fear and Greed Clues

Fear manifests itself in the form of procrastination. Procrastination is rife, with many would-be investors delaying the purchase of property as they wait for a better time to arrive. This procrastination creates a pipeline of potential buyers who will typically end up buying during the boom, because by then property would have proven itself to them as a good investment vehicle. There is very low confidence in the property market as many are still fearful of property investment – the last slump is still fresh in their minds. Greed is hardly evident at all because the fear of making a mistake is much greater in the market than the desire to make potential financial gains.

Media Clues

At this time newspaper headlines indicate that there is a shortage of property to rent and therefore rents are rapidly increasing. Typically there is some scepticism that the current pace of property value and rental growth can continue.

Actions of the Wise Investor

Wise property investors will enter an aggressive buying pattern at this part of the property cycle to ensure they maximise the growth of their portfolio's cashflow and equity position. But they will still ensure that each property delivers a positive cashflow. The wise investor will typically purchase properties in upper socio-economic locations that deliver a positive cashflow. They will also be open to purchasing properties in these locations which require significant deferred maintenance which will be attended to immediately upon purchase. This guarantees higher rent and subsequently a stronger cashflow while maximising any value increase to be achieved in the coming boom.

The Middle of the Recovery

This stage of the recovery is evidenced by strong returns on property investment. Many inexperienced investors will sell former property investments made at the end of the last boom, to recover their initial purchase price, because they fear current values may be unsustainable.

The key drivers at this point reveal strong returns on investment in property, property vacancy rates continuing to fall, property construction levels starting to increase and affordability levels remaining high. Gentrification of property becomes the flavour of the day and previously deferred maintenance now takes priority. Building service companies experience a mini-boom on the back of what appears to be a sudden increased demand for their services.

> 'House price growth is usually hesitant and uneven during this stage, as confusion reigns over whether the current level of growth can continue or not.'

Fear and Greed Clues

Fear still has a grip on the majority of potential property investors. Many will be reluctant to invest at this time and will want further evidence that property will be a good investment. Greed remains subdued.

Media Clues

Newspaper headlines revolve around the fact it is now more cost-effective to own property than to rent it. However there is much confusion over whether property is actually a good investment or not, with many commentators pointing to the low returns and value erosion experienced in the preceding years of the property slump.

Actions of the Wise Investor

The wise investors will continue their aggressive buying pattern to ensure they maximise the growth of their portfolio. Their focus will be to ensure that each property purchase delivers a positive cashflow. They will still seek out the best located quality property they can find and/or property with significant deferred maintenance. Now that land values are showing signs of increasing, they will also seek to buy land in good quality areas if they can build on it and still achieve a positive cashflow.

The End of the Recovery

This stage of the recovery is difficult to identify as there is little change in the key drivers. However the major key drivers to watch at this point are the reducing returns achieved on any new investment in property as values start to outpace rental increases, and the number of people per household starting to increase as rising rents begin to impact on the affordability of renting. Property starts to look like an attractive investment vehicle to more and more potential investors. By contrast, it becomes less affordable as a result of increasing values. Property prices will surge upward at this stage.

Fear and Greed Clues

While this is still an optimum time to buy property, fear still grips many people who avoid investing because memories of the painful former slump phase are still fresh in their minds. Fear is not as widespread as it was, but many are still nervous. Greed is still subdued.

Media Clues

Headlines referring to property value increases start to appear, and many property market observers mistakenly believe that the property boom began when the market entered the beginning of the recovery phase, citing value increases as evidence of the boom (refer to Graph 7.1).

Other commentators dispute that a boom exists or will even eventuate.

Actions of the Wise Investor

Now that land values are increasing in the better locations it is difficult to purchase property in those locations that achieves a positive cashflow. The wise investor will still seek to purchase property and do-ups in the best mid- to high socio-economic locations they can afford. They will also seek land in these locations where they can build property and still achieve a positive cashflow. Wise investors know that this is still a good time to build, because land values will continue to increase throughout the coming boom phase and the cost of building at this time has not yet seen a strong upward trend. It is also still relatively easy to find skilled labour to build houses so the construction time is minimised.

Key Drivers in the Recovery

Peaks and Troughs of Key Drivers During the Recovery

	RECOVERY		
	Beginning	Middle	End
DEMOGRAPHIC			
Net Migration/Population Growth	+	+	+
Property Vacancy Rates	–	–	–
Employment	+	+	+
Property Construction	Trough	+	+
No. of People per Household	–	Trough	+
FINANCIAL			
Property ROI	+	Peak	–
Rents	+	+	+
Incomes	+	+	+
Property Finance Availability	+	+	+
Gross Domestic Product	+	Peak	–
Property Values	+	+	+
Property Affordability	Peak	–	–
EMOTIONAL			
No. of Days to Sell Property	–	–	–
Gentrification	Trough	+	+
Property Listings	–	–	–
Property Sales	+	+	+

Key

Peak	=	When a key driver is at its highest point, just before it begins to decline
Trough	=	When a key driver is at its lowest point, just before it begins to rise
+	=	Increase in key driver
–	=	Decrease in key driver
ROI	=	Return on investment

(Refer to appendices for a list of all key driver peaks and troughs throughout a complete cycle.)

CHAPTER SUMMARY

- The recovery is an exciting but short phase of the property cycle. It offers a wealth of opportunity but is not easily recognised by most investors. Property values start to rise relatively sharply during the recovery.

- At the beginning of the recovery, the population begins to increase and subsequently rents start to rise rapidly, almost taking the market by surprise. Suddenly it seems there is a shortage of available property to rent compared with the many people who seem to be in the market. Property values start to rise at single-digit levels (under 10%) on an annualised basis.

- By the middle of the recovery, property starts to increase in favour as an investment vehicle. Property is generally affordable and returns from property investment are attractive. Building service companies start to see a strong lift in demand.

- The end of the recovery is evidenced by reducing return on any new investment in property as values start to outpace rental increases. Property starts to become less affordable.

- Throughout the recovery phase the prevailing motivating emotion is fear whereas greed is subdued.

Chapter 8

The Boom Phase

The boom is the most exciting phase of the property cycle for inexperienced property investors but is not so exciting for seasoned

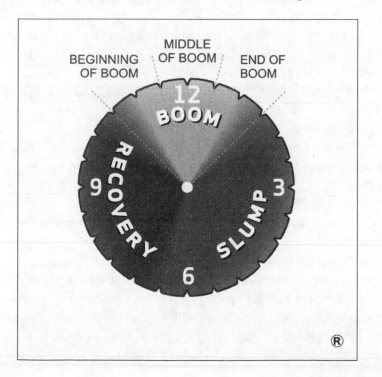

investors, who find the late slump and early recovery phases offer better opportunities. Many of the key drivers of the property cycle will peak near the end of the boom phase. The entire boom phase usually passes relatively quickly compared with the slump. However if the boom is extended in spite of many of the key drivers peaking, then it will most likely eventually be offset by a longer slump phase and/or by potential value decreases during the slump. In other words: the longer and stronger the boom, the greater the likelihood of a more severe downturn during the inevitable slump.

> 'When the boom lasts longer than it should, it is a bit like going to a party and having such a great time that you wish it would never end.'

So you stay out later and later, enjoying the party until it is well into the next morning. You finally realise that you are exhausted and cannot party any longer, so you go home to get some rest. However when you finally wake up later that day you wish you had left the party hours earlier because now you are suffering the consequences of being out so late. Most property investors wish the party time of the property cycle, the boom, would never end – but as surely as night follows day it will. It's just a matter of when . . .

If the key drivers indicate the boom should be over but the party is still in full swing, then you can expect a severe slump to eventually follow.

Economic times are good during the boom. The reason economic times remain good is in part because property represents the largest financial investment that the majority of people make. Rising prices make property owners feel richer, in fact much richer, with many property investors dreaming of retirement in just a few short years!

Increases in property prices also have a significant impact on consumer spending. Consumers will borrow against their newfound property wealth to upgrade their lifestyle with new furniture, appliances, cars, boats, holidays and holiday homes.

In this chapter you will learn to interpret the evidence shown by the key drivers and the clues given by the media at each stage of the boom. You will also learn how fear and greed influence people's actions throughout the boom, and contribute to the downfall of many property investors.

The New Zealand boom of the mid-1990s saw a new wave of property investors in the form of the baby boomers. These investors had been disillusioned with the lacklustre performance of super-annuation schemes and managed funds during the early 1990s. They were also still nervous about investing in shares as the sharemarket crash of 1987 remained fresh in their minds. Property investment looked 'as safe as houses'. They flocked to investment seminars to learn all about the benefits of purchasing property using a concept called negative gearing.

> 'Negative gearing is the term used to describe a situation where the property investment does not make enough money (from rental income) to cover the expenses involved in keeping that investment.'

As a result of making a loss by owning this property, you receive a tax benefit you can use to offset against any tax paid on other income you receive. You lose money by owning the property but the tax department offsets some of that loss for you.

Armed with this knowledge the baby boomers invested heavily in property to build wealth to enjoy in their retirement. But many of these investors commenced purchasing their property investments in 1996 when the boom was nearly over.

The concept of negative gearing has been promoted as a legiti-mate way to get the tax department to help you pay off your property purchases. It was not until the slump of the late 1990s that many investors came to understand the folly of negative gearing.

The Beginning of the Boom

The key drivers of the property cycle at the beginning of the boom include continued strong growth in net migration and/or net population growth, increasing employment levels, increasing rents and increasing income levels.

This first stage of the boom produces increasing returns for property owners in the form of higher rents and growing equity in their property, as values increase on an annualised basis by higher percentages than recently experienced during the recovery. Ironically, this stage of the boom also produces falling returns on any new investment in property. This is because more and more people enter the property market which typically causes property values to increase faster than rental values, thereby reducing returns on property investments.

Public seminars about property investing are prominently advertised at the beginning of the boom. These seminars are often run by self-proclaimed experts who will extol the virtues of property as an investment vehicle.

Fear and Greed Clues

Typically there is still some hesitancy among the general public about investing at this stage of the boom due to a fear that property may not prove to be a wise investment. Many investors want more hard evidence that values will continue to rise before they begin investing or speculating. Greed is still not prevalent but there are signs that it is about to take hold. There is increasing anecdotal evidence of capital gains achieved by people who have recently bought and sold property.

Media Clues

Contradictory newspaper headlines appear that one day praise property as a meritorious investment, and the next day are highly sceptical of its continued potential for capital growth.

Actions of the Wise Investor

At this stage wise investors will be alert to the signals the media is giving about property to the general public. Wise investors will seek to take advantage of any negative press about property, by consistently making offers to purchase positive cashflow property typically in lower to middle socio-economic locations. This is because the wise investor understands that sooner or later in this early stage of the boom, negative press will have an influence on some existing property owners and investors. These property owners and investors will believe that it is a good time to sell their property, but they will sell for a price that may not reflect the current market value of the property. The wise investor still demands a positive cashflow from newly acquired property and will most likely find property that meets this criterion in less desirable areas. This is still a good time to build, because land values will continue to increase throughout the boom and the cost of building will not yet be subject to strong upward pressure. It is also still relatively easy to find skilled labour to build property at this time.

The Middle of the Boom

At this stage of the boom many of the key drivers starting to peak.

These key drivers include net migration and/or net population increases and high rents. Such key drivers reach unsustainable levels and subsequently become due for a correction. Many other key drivers show continued increases such as employment levels, incomes, construction levels and property sales volumes.

Other key drivers are nearing their lowest levels or troughs. For example, property vacancy rates reach extremely low levels as tenants queue up for property to rent. The number of days to sell property reduces as property sells rapidly and the volume of property listed for sale diminishes.

Property finance is easy to qualify for, with the option to purchase property with very little or even no cash deposit. Many second-tier lenders such as finance companies and non-banks will become overly generous with their lending policies, but will charge higher interest rates than traditional lenders, and sometimes large upfront fees.

An increasing number of first-time property investors enter the market with the purchase of their first property investment.

Values of property rise at this stage of the boom at a similar pace to that experienced in the beginning stage of the boom. The number of tenants defaulting on rent payments increases as rents start to become unsustainably high.

This stage of the boom is relatively easy to recognise because the hype surrounding property investment gathers pace. It seems like everyone has a success story of generating wealth from property investment, or at least knows someone else who has.

Get-rich-quick seminars become more popular proclaiming that you too can be a millionaire or even a multi-millionaire! Speakers will include the likes of former employees who will tell you they used to be slaves to their employers, working from payday to payday for little financial reward, but that now they have become seriously rich in a few short years by investing in property. You can join them and all you have to do is pay them handsomely for their knowledge or attend their two- to three-day seminar for just a few thousand dollars! Don't believe it for a moment. While a small percentage of investors sometimes generate much wealth rapidly, the financial ruin eventually left behind in the slump by many amateurs trying to get rich quick is serious, devastating and lasts a long time. Many get-rich-quick merchants appear in boom times and then disappear in the slump with a fistful of dollars in their hands, leaving a sour taste in the mouths of many who believed their so-called wisdom.

Forced property sales (mortgagee sales) are few and far between at this stage of the cycle. Certain suburbs within cities will emerge as potential hot spots as they will have missed out on the full impact of the current wave of capital growth. Such undervalued pockets of property always emerge during this stage of the boom. This may arise for a number of reasons, such as a lack of recent sales within an area. There may be few comparable sales within the locality on which potential vendors can base an assessment of value, so their assessment may be made on earlier sales at lower values with little regard to the present level of demand. Another reason can be the general perception that the suburb is the least sought-after area within a region, therefore little capital growth is expected. These undesirable areas though will still experience capital growth due to relativity – values in that suburb should increase by a similar proportion to values in the immediately surrounding areas. It may be justified that the suburb experiences a lower growth but sometimes this growth becomes disproportionately low temporarily compared with the surrounding suburbs, marking a potential hot spot.

Fear and Greed Clues

This is the time when greed becomes evident. Many people are motivated to invest because of the false belief that the more properties they buy, the closer they will get to financial freedom. Greed also appears in its most potent form – that of speculation. Speculation seems to be the path to easy riches, with rapid capital growth giving rise to the ridiculous expectation that 'you can't lose'.

Media Clues

Newspaper headlines state the boom is in full swing, but often also indicate that it may be over or is nearly over. Confusion prevails over whether the bullish run on property values can continue. Many economists predict that values have peaked and the property market is about to cool off.

There are stories of unaffordable rental levels and people being unable to ever afford to purchase a property. Property investment is a hot topic in many publications which feature advice on various aspects of investing for the aspiring property investor.

Actions of the Wise Investor

Wise investors will still be interested only in property that offers a positive cashflow. Unfortunately there will be a genuine lack of sound opportunities to purchase such property at this time. To create positive cashflow from property purchases usually involves implementing strategies to generate additional cashflow from already owned properties or newly acquired property. For example in the New Zealand boom of the 1970s, many wise investors achieved this result by converting older homes into two or more separate rentable units.

In the current boom of 2004, the opportunity to build 'minor dwellings' has proven a smart strategy, allowing investors to secure two incomes for the price of one and a half! This strategy creates positive cashflow from what may formerly have been a negative cash-flow property. (For more on positive cashflow refer to Chapter 11.)

The End of the Boom

At this stage of the boom many of the key drivers have reached their peak.

Population growth has now reversed its upward trend, vacancy rates slowly start to increase, and subsequently rents start to fall. Income growth also looks set to peak and it starts taking a little longer to sell property. Construction levels are high and cranes are commonplace on the skyline. Property becomes less affordable than it has been as a result of high property values. Property finance remains relatively easy to qualify for, as financial institutions strive to meet ever-increasing lending budgets while they rapidly grow their mortgage lending book. Some second-tier lenders will still be aggressively lending at high interest rates. Creative financing facilities will become available, making it easier than ever to borrow for that property purchase. Property renovations become overcapitalisations as people spend too much.

Property values will surge and may rise faster at this part of the boom than they did in the beginning and middle of the boom. Unfortunately much of the growth in value sustained during this part of the boom may be eroded during the coming slump. While it is true that some house price indices such as the Australian and the USA indices reveal no actual decrease in house prices during the slump phase of the 1990s (refer to Graph 1.3 and 1.4), that does not mean that no property was sold at a loss during the slump. It just means that the majority of property sales reflected increases.

The property investment seminars which sprang into prominence at the beginning of the boom now abound in plague-like proportions. Often these seminars are promoted by construction and property companies with vested interests in selling their own product, namely negatively geared property. Many inexperienced investors will be lured to these seminars by the promise of learning how to get rich quick.

> 'This is the time when many inexperienced property investors begin, or keep on, buying property in the belief that values will continue to climb.'

What these investors do not realise is that there is an inevitable correction coming in the next phase of the property cycle (the slump). Investors dominate the market and drive property prices beyond the reach of many potential first-home buyers.

The end of the boom is typically not a good time to buy. Unfortunately it is also typically the time when a multitude of new investors start entering the market and buying their first and sometimes subsequent investment properties. This influx of new investors seems to be driven by a widely held belief that property will continue to perform as a superior investment vehicle because of its track record of good performance during the early and middle stages of the boom. Investors will typically overestimate property values at this end stage of the boom.

Some of the reasons cited as to why this boom will continue include:

- Property is the world's biggest asset class therefore will always be in demand. (But obviously if there is too much property then supply can outweigh demand.)

- There is a shortage of land and they are not making any more land, so property prices will keep rising. (Of course little account is taken of the fact that new land can, and is, created all over the world every day. This new land is in the form of airspace or even landfill over rivers or the sea. Buildings can obviously be built up for several, or even dozens, of floors, thereby effectively multiplying the amount of land available on the ground. Interestingly, the shortage of land in Hong Kong has not resulted in ever-increasing prices . . .)

• We have restrictive planning laws which will limit the supply of new property to the market. (Attempts to curtail supply, such as through restrictive planning laws, will temporarily impact on the availability of new housing but this is no guarantee of continued increases in value and laws can always be changed . . .)

• Population increases alone will continue to create adequate demand to fuel price increases. (Unfortunately even population increases alone will not necessarily result in ever-increasing property prices because this also depends on how much property is available to house such a population increase. The USA has experienced much faster population growth than the UK from 1980–2000, yet real house prices in the USA have risen much less over that time than in the UK.)

There will also be stories told around this time that the only reasons former property booms did not last was because banks increased interest rates, adversely affecting affordability and creating the perfect environment to end the boom. But if that is the case, who forgot to point this out to Germany and Japan who have had low interest rates but have still seen property values decrease or languish throughout the 1990s? In fact low interest rates in Japan were the cause for significant over-investment in property during the 1980s, resulting in property values decreasing significantly over the 1990s.

'Many investors will mistakenly believe that this boom will continue, because of what on the surface appear to be sound arguments such as lower interest rates justifying a higher value in comparison to rental returns.'

But if this were the case then a typically highly leveraged investment like property needs to experience only a small increase in interest rates to detrimentally affect its value very quickly. In these times of flexible financing we can often borrow 100% for property purchases, which increases our exposure to potential losses. Let's say interest rates are 4% p.a. and the value of $200,000 applies to a house earning a net yield of $4,000 or 2% p.a. (net return is after all expenses including interest costs based on 100% financing). If indeed reduced interest rates do influence the value of this house, then it can be argued that if interest rates decreased to 3.5% p.a. the same net required return of 2% p.a. would mean the house would have a value of $250,000. However if interest rates increased to 4.5% p.a., then the same required net return of 2% p.a. would mean the value would decrease to $150,000.

We all know that house prices are not typically this volatile, but what is disturbing is the number of property investors who, faced with higher interest rates and therefore a decreased return, will quickly recount the capital growth prospects of property. These investors will indicate that the expected capital growth will give them a more-than-adequate return to justify current prices. Beginner property investors are encouraged to disregard the level of net return achieved and instead focus on the long-term prospects of capital growth. The problem is that many investors will not own their property investments for the long term as the slump eventually wears many of them down.

The surge of activity and blatant disregard for basic investment fundamentals seen at the end of the boom creates a recipe for disaster as property values spiral into orbit.

Many investors consider that they are not paying too much for their property purchase at this time because they could always sell it at a profit. The bigger fool theory is the belief that if the price you are prepared to pay for a property establishes that property's value, then someone else will be prepared to pay more for that property than you have. Even if you have been somewhat foolish and did pay too much, you believe that there will always be a bigger fool than you who is prepared to pay even more than you have. The problem is that some investors will eventually become the biggest fools themselves when the market slumps. Only then will they realise there is no longer any bigger fool prepared to pay more than they did.

Of course if they simply don't sell the property for another property cycle or two they will most likely still make money from owning it, but many of the biggest fools will take a loss in the coming slump.

With property prices reaching peak levels in relation to incomes, home buyers and some investors start to be effectively priced out of the market.

Fear and Greed Clues

At this stage of the boom, fear takes a back seat as greed becomes the prominent motivation for investors. Generally greed is in the ascendant and is apparent in many investment transactions that are speculative. Many short-term investors buy and then on-sell property for a quick profit. This form of speculation helps fuel the boom to its ultimate demise.

Many new property construction projects are sold off the plans (that is, before they are built) with extremely low initial deposits required, and these opportunities attract speculators who intend to sell the property before or at completion. Sometimes these purchases are on-sold several times before completion, with each on-seller realising a profit and thereby fuelling price rises even further. There are a large number of people buying purely for the expectation of capital gains – but expected capital gains are no guarantee of actual value increases.

Because of the present lack of fear of taking financial risks by investing, combined with the need of so many people to feed their greed, this is the time when alternative investments are heavily promoted to those who have already benefited from the property boom. These investments will often (but not always) be related to property in some way, so they appear to be similar but offer much better returns than the mediocre levels now seen in traditional property investment. Good examples of these types of investment are property syndications or property timeshares. There will also be many other investment opportunities touted which offer far superior short-term returns than property with apparently little risk or effort attached. Unfortunately these investments are usually highly risky, such as margin or arbitrage trading of anything from shares and foreign exchange currencies to commodities like oil, silver and gold. While these can still be valid investment vehicles many investors will lose money through such high-risk plays.

> 'This is also the stage of the cycle when property investors are most vulnerable to unscrupulous investment schemes and straight-out scams.'

Property investors have created a lot of wealth in the preceding boom, so of course they become easy targets for scams.

In the late 1990s one of these scams, called Investors International, was promoted in New Zealand to property investors as a quicker way to get rich. This scheme promised massive returns of 15% per month compounding, with little risk. To learn more about this opportunity you had to attend a week-long offshore seminar with a number of credible guest speakers, many of whom had no idea that Investors International was a scam. The scheme even promoted the opportunity to earn tax-free returns. Of course many people like the idea of outsmarting the tax system even if they usually end up outsmarting themselves. Sure enough, the scheme was soon uncovered as a scam, but not soon enough to stop many investors from losing a lot of money.

You must guard yourself from greed vigilantly at this time or you can easily lose some of your recently created property wealth. Remember: when faced with so-called investment opportunities at this time, if it sounds too good to be true it probably is!

Vendors also fall prey to greed at this stage of the property cycle as they attempt to maximise the sale price they can achieve. I saw a good example of this recently when a friend of mine, John, was attempting to purchase an investment property.

The property was being marketed by the vendors as a private sale without a price. The vendors were considering selling it at auction but were interested in offers. It was a multiple-income-producing property and John made an offer of $625,000, which was equivalent to a sale price (before agent fees) of around $650,000 if the vendor had used a real estate agent to sell it. The vendor then sought advice from their local real estate agent who advised the property should easily get a higher sale price at auction.

John had undertaken some research which revealed the vendor had paid only $330,000 for the property seven years earlier. The vendor could have made a profit of $295,000 but decided that they could get more at an auction.

By the time the property went to auction John had pursued another opportunity and was no longer in a position to buy it. There was only one bid at the auction of $480,000 which was actually made by my another friend of mine, James. The auctioneer spoke with James and said the property obviously has a much higher market value than his bid, and an attempt was made to get James to increase his offer. James correctly advised the agent that the market had already spoken and the value of the property was indeed only $480,000; otherwise someone else would have made a higher bid. The auction had been preceded by an extensive marketing campaign and the market had had ample opportunity to consider its value, then advise the agent of such value by bidding at the auction. The fact that the vendor had previously had an offer of $625,000 meant nothing to James. The auction failed to conclude in a sale.

Needless to say the vendors would have had to pay for the costs of the failed auction and the property remains on the market. This is a classic case of vendor greed. The offer of $625,000 was indeed a fair one at the time it was made, and in hindsight the vendor must regret not accepting it.

Media Clues

At the end of the boom various commentators will extol the superior virtues of this particular boom and explain why it is so different from every other boom ever seen, suggesting that it should never end. Some economists predict that values will continue to increase for quite some time, and the public are encouraged to buy now or miss out forever on the opportunity. Other economists will also warn of impending doom and the coming collapse of the property market because the fundamentals of current property prices are not sound. Many media articles revolve around the question of whether the boom is actually over yet or not.

Actions of the Wise Investor

The wise investor will enter a holding pattern at this part of the property cycle. They will focus on ensuring their current property portfolio is robust enough to survive the coming slump. They will add value to their existing portfolio to increase its rentability, and thus ensure adequate cashflow can be generated to support borrowings in the event that rents decrease and interest rates increase significantly.

Their key focus is to ensure their financial position will be adequate for the survival of the rest of their portfolio through the coming slump.

They will consider selling some of their portfolio at this stage. The reasons they may sell are varied. One reason will be to strengthen their financial position for the coming slump so they are able to accumulate more property at cheaper prices if values fall. That way they can ensure they have the opportunity to be countercyclical, because they will be in a position to buy when many other investors are trying to sell.

Another reason they may sell is to dispose of their worst-performing property, property which carries too much downside risk or property with significant ongoing maintenance costs which affect the financial viability of holding such property over the long term. The wise investor may also sell some property at this stage to free up cash for diversification into other investment vehicles or even to fund some lifestyle choices.

As they did in the middle of the boom, the wise investor will consider the potential of renovations to add to an existing property's income stream in order to generate positive cashflow or to create another income stream from their existing property portfolio, although they will find that building materials and labour costs are high at this time due to the present strong level of building demand which may make such plans unattractive financially.

KEY DRIVERS IN THE BOOM

Peaks and Troughs of Key Drivers During the Boom

	BOOM		
	Beginning	Middle	End
DEMOGRAPHIC			
Net Migration/Population Growth	+	Peak	–
Property Vacancy Rates	–	–	Trough
Employment	+	+	Peak
Property Construction	+	+	Peak
No. of People per Household	+	+	+
FINANCIAL			
Property ROI	–	–	–
Rents	+	Peak	–
Incomes	+	+	Peak
Property Finance Availability	+	+	Peak
Gross Domestic Product	–	–	–
Property Values	+	+	+
Property Affordability	–	–	–
EMOTIONAL			
No. of Days to Sell Property	–	–	Trough
Gentrification	+	+	Peak
Property Listings	–	Trough	+
Property Sales	+	+	Peak

Key

Peak = When a key driver is at its highest point, just before it begins to decline

Trough = When a key diver is at its lowest point, just before it begins to rise

+ = Increase in key driver

– = Decrease in key driver

ROI = Return on investment

(Refer to appendices for a list of all key driver peaks and troughs throughout a complete cycle.)

CHAPTER SUMMARY

• The period from the beginning to the end of the boom usually passes quickly in relation to the slump, but if the boom is extended then it will eventually be offset by a longer slump phase accompanied by greater value decreases during the slump than would normally occur.

• The beginning of the boom provides increasing returns from already owned property investments but decreasing returns on newly acquired property investments.

• The middle and end of the boom are evidenced by the activity levels of many of the key drivers starting to peak, and a change in direction of several other key drivers as they start to decrease.

• Many key drivers reach their peak in the boom.

• At the beginning of the boom the prevailing motivating emotion is fear but by the end of the boom greed prevails.

• Avoid speculation and guard yourself from greed at this time or you can easily lose some of your recently created property wealth.

Chapter 9

The Slump Phase

The slump is a difficult phase of the property cycle. Many inexperienced investors misunderstand the slump and believe property

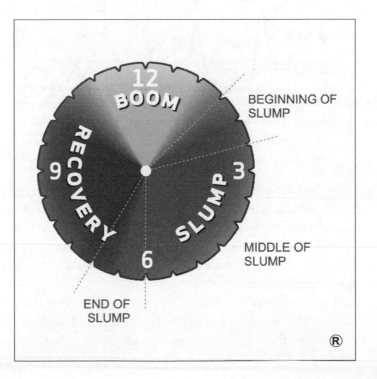

prices will crash instantly when the market enters this phase. But the market usually experiences a slow landing before the slump inevitably bites. This slow landing is so gradual that most property investors don't realise it is taking place until it ultimately affects them in the form of lower rental levels and a plateau and/or a reduction in property values. Also because values do still increase, albeit marginally, throughout some (if not all) of the slump, the majority of property investors do not even realise it has begun until long after it has actually commenced.

Prior to the 1990s, slumps in the New Zealand property cycle did not result in negative nominal growth. However since 1990 we have had occasions where negative growth has occurred, as shown in Graph 9.1 below.

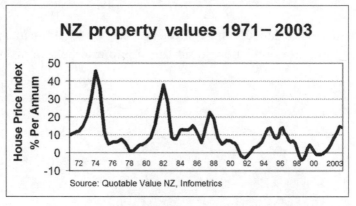

Graph 9.1

When the last slump in New Zealand commenced in 1997 many people started to seek advice from my company because their circumstances had been adversely affected by the decrease in property values.

Typically, they had overcommitted by buying as many properties as they could in the vain hope that the more property they had the better off they would be.

One couple really surprised me. They were clients of my company, and told me they were having difficulty meeting all their mortgage payments and they would like me to advise them what to do. I reviewed their file before our scheduled meeting. I found that they had good personal incomes, a satisfactory level of rental income and not too much mortgage debt. I thought at the time that perhaps one of them was no longer employed, which might explain their financial hardship. I also noted they had started investing with the intention of accumulating ten properties in ten years. Their plan was to then sell five of them, which hopefully would give them adequate cash to retain the other five properties without mortgages.

When they met with me the first thing they said was, 'Kieran, we have a confession to make.' I didn't quite know what to expect next, but they went on to explain that they had not been 100% honest with the banks they had borrowed from and had failed to disclose another four rental properties they owned, all mortgaged to a different bank. They also told me they had both left their jobs to become full-time property dealers. Their intention was to buy properties that required renovating; they would spend a significant amount on renovations and then resell the property at a profit. They thought the boom would never end . . . Until they had to sell their first renovated property for a loss of $20,000!

At the same time interest rates were increasing, which meant higher monthly mortgage payments. Rents had also decreased as a result of increased vacancy rates because of over-construction in the boom, so they were getting less rent from their rental portfolio. They were receiving total annual rental income of $144,000 but their total mortgage commitments were $156,000, plus they had living expenses of $72,000 which included ownership costs of all of their rentals. They were clearly overcommitted financially with a monthly shortfall of $7,000, but they had also experienced some really bad luck – the tenants of one of their properties had had to be evicted for unpaid rent of thousands of dollars and they had maliciously damaged the property before vacating it. To top it all off, the values of their properties were less than they thought. The property market had changed considerably and they were now definitely in trouble. Panicked by their circumstances, they asked what I thought they should do.

It was some of the hardest advice I have ever had to give. They had no choice but to sell some of their property and reduce their debt levels by at least $400,000, and both seek employment. I cautiously suggested they should sell their beach house but they couldn't bear to do this, and decided they would live there rather than in their family home. So the next option was to sell their family home, which they reluctantly agreed to do. They also agreed to seek employment and shelve their plans to be property dealers. They believed the anecdotal evidence of property values which indicated that they should never sell their investments, so they had done whatever they could to retain their rental portfolio.

To their credit, these clients took the advice well. They sold their family home and both found employment to reduce their financial burden. They retained the rest of their portfolio of twelve rentals. They were able to maintain ownership of their portfolio in the ensuing years, and today have both a sound portfolio and their own family home again. They have learned from their mistakes.

They are the lucky ones. There were many property investors who lost massive amounts by falling prey to greed during the boom, only to lose their newfound wealth when the slump eventually took its toll. Not all these investors struggled simply as a result of failing to disclose their full financial position to their financiers. Many suffered from a combination of events which led to them being under financial pressure. There is such a strong demand from investors for help during the slump that my company offers a 'property cycle survival pack' service to assess investors' financial status and make recommendations on how they can restructure their affairs to survive financially.

'The slump can be an excellent time for those financially prepared to take advantage of the opportunities that will eventually become apparent at the middle and end stages of the phase.'

However many investors find their financial position is so detrimentally affected by the slump that further investment in property is neither possible from a financial perspective, nor a priority. Most investors will find their borrowing capacity will be significantly adversely affected by the slump as rents decrease and values plateau or even decrease.

The Beginning of the Slump

At this stage of the slump there are continued increasing vacancy rates as a result of an oversupply of rental accommodation, and subsequently decreasing returns from existing property investments in the form of reducing rents. Property affordability has now been detrimentally affected due to high values and financiers redefining their lending criteria. Ironically, property values continue to increase, albeit more slowly than in the previous boom. Rents decrease, clearly at odds with values which continue to rise. While values still seem to rise, albeit at single-digit levels (under 10%), in this early part of the slump such rises are generally restricted to the least desirable areas; values in the more desirable areas start to falter. Current values are unlikely to be sustained in the medium term due to the large amount of new property under construction. This new property has a significant lead-time before it is completed, and demand will fall before the new supply is available. A surplus of property will result in downward pressure on prices. This is due to competition with much newly built and existing property on the market at a time when fewer and fewer buyers are in the market.

The more severe the oversupply of property, the more severe any eventual correction in values will be.

Fear and Greed Clues

Fear begins to creep into the hearts of property investors as they realise that the boom may soon be just a memory. But greed still has a firm hold on many investors, who refuse to accept the truth and rather like to point out that property has had a stellar performance over the past few years. These investors feel secure in the false belief that their financial position will remain sound. Typically, many inexperienced property investors believe values will rebound with a vengeance in spite of falling returns.

Media Clues

This stage of the slump is usually accompanied by newspaper headlines indicating property prices are too high and are overdue for a correction. Some experts will be naively (or with vested interests) singing the praises of property, reassuring investors that the market will soon rebound, with investors seeing similar growth in values to that experienced in the preceding few years.

Wise Investors' Actions

Wise property investors continue to position themselves to be countercyclical, by ensuring they are financially able to accumulate more property even though they will not be in a rush to buy at this point in the property cycle. They will observe a shift in the market, as property loses favour as an investment vehicle. They will be poised to take advantage of opportunities to purchase newly constructed property in forced sale situations (such as mortgagee sales), and so will secure a positive cashflow.

Wise investors are still reluctant buyers and their criteria for purchasing property will still be to achieve a good positive cashflow. They will not utilise all their borrowing capacity at this stage because they know the next stage of the slump will produce even better opportunities.

The Middle of the Slump

The key drivers at this point include property vacancy rates reaching a peak with many vacant dwellings, and the low returns on property investment slowly starting to bite. Property is now clearly out of favour as an investment vehicle. As people struggle financially under the pressure of reduced cashflows and decreasing or stalling values, forced property sales become commonplace. Deferred property maintenance is common due to a lack of cashflow or willingness to invest more into properties that are providing poor returns. It seems that everyone has a horror story of losing wealth from property investment, or at least everyone knows someone else who has lost money from investing in property.

At this time a lot of people wish they had never started investing in property. Many will be suffering financial hardship and will struggle to cope emotionally with their deteriorating financial position. Relatively new entrants to property investment will tend to give up and sell their property at a loss, to be free of the stress they face as a result of the collapse in value of what they thought were wise investments.

Fear and Greed Clues

Now is the time when the fear of failure becomes evident in property investment. It is reinforced daily with stories of people making significant losses from property. This fear quickly translates into panic, especially if there are some market influencers also impacting on property, such as increasing interest rates. Many property investors will sell down their property, fearful that they may lose even more if they keep their property longer. Others will simply be resigned to waiting until values recover before they can sell to recoup their initial investment.

Greed starts to become subdued as it becomes clear that the days of quick property profits are over for now.

Media Clues

This stage is relatively easy to recognise because newspaper headlines commonly reinforce the fact it is now cheaper to rent than to own property. Other headlines include the *I told you so!* stories about the demise of property as an investment. These stories are usually written by advisors who promote investment vehicles other than property.

Bad press about the unsustainability of current property values takes centre stage in media headlines. Home buyers refuse to pay the perceived high level of prices, and in light of the low yields experienced by property investors, combined with declining expectations of capital growth, many investors will attempt to sell some or all of their property investments. The lack of buyers means that values can move into freefall. The realisation that property is an illiquid investment becomes blatantly and painfully apparent.

Wise Investors' Actions

Due to the surplus of well-priced property opportunities at this time, the wise investor will seek out the keenest vendors they can find (or forced sale situations) in middle socio-economic locations. The wise investor will be highly selective and only commit to those opportunities which produce a sound positive cashflow.

The End of the Slump

At this stage of the slump several of the key drivers reach troughs at around the same time.

Net migration levels and employment growth is low. Rents become stable as well as incomes, property values, the number of property sales and the number of days it takes to sell. The property market lacks direction, and property investment becomes noticeable by its absence from advisors' recommendations. Values typically falter and fall further than they had earlier in the slump and property investment becomes an unpopular subject to talk about. Gross Domestic Product and property affordability have slowly been improving throughout the slump.

> 'While this is the optimum time to buy, most people avoid investing in property because it has proven to be such a bad investment in the past few years as the property cycle has progressed through the slump phase.'

Property investors generally underestimate property values at this end stage of the slump, and many pay little heed to existing sound fundamentals such as an increasing return on investment.

A few of the reasons given as to why this is not a good time to buy will include:

- Property has proved to be an inferior investment vehicle to shares and bonds over recent years. (Of course property looks like an inferior investment when you are considering its performance as an asset class during the slump phase of the property cycle.)

- In these times we will most likely have a low-inflation environment. This means real house price growth will remain only nominal because inflation is a major component of house price growth. (Even in the presence of low inflation there is evidence that house price growth can still be significant – see Graph 6.2 of New Zealand inflation versus house price growth in Chapter 6.)

- We don't have an adequate population inflow to create a strong increase in demand, which would result in additional properties or strong upward pressure on property values. (Population increases can occur dramatically and quickly place upward pressure on values in the absence of adequate supply.)

There will also be claims at this time that the only reason former property booms occurred was because interest rates were low, increasing affordability and creating the perfect environment to start a boom. As mentioned in Chapter 6, interest rate levels do not always impact on property values.

Many investors will mistakenly believe that this particular slump will never end and that the boom days are gone forever, because of what on the surface appear to be sound arguments. But about now some property investors will again wisely start to regard the level of net return achieved on any property purchases as being of paramount importance, and pay little heed to the long-term prospects of capital growth in their purchasing decisions.

With property prices starting to reach realistic levels in relation to incomes, first-home buyers begin to enter the market as the dream of owning their own home finally becomes a reality again. Property finance starts to become easier to qualify for, and property becomes much more affordable.

Fear and Greed Clues

The fear of a repeat of former losses or of uncomfortable times keeps most people from investing in property at this time. Greed is hardly evident at all as fear is the prevailing motivator.

Media Clues

Property is not a popular topic right now, so not much is said about it. Any news relating to property is typically bad news, and other investment classes' performances are favourably compared to the poor returns from property over recent years.

Wise Investors' Actions

At this time wise investors know the slump may still last for quite some time, so the positive cashflow generated from any property investments must still justify any further investment. They will shift their focus to quality property and do-ups with character or charm in upper socio-economic locations and around the CBD fringe.

KEY DRIVERS IN THE SLUMP

Peaks and Troughs of Key Drivers During the Slump

| | **SLUMP** | | |
---	Beginning	Middle	End
DEMOGRAPHIC			
Net Migration/Population Growth	–	Trough	+
Property Vacancy Rates	+	Peak	–
Employment	–	–	Trough
Property Construction	–	–	–
No. of People per Household	Peak	–	–
FINANCIAL			
Property ROI	–	Trough	+
Rents	–	–	Trough
Incomes	–	–	Trough
Property Finance Availability	–	–	Trough
Gross Domestic Product	Trough	+	+
Property Values	Peak	–	Trough
Property Affordability	Trough	+	+
EMOTIONAL			
No. of Days To Sell Property	+	+	Peak
Gentrification	–	–	–
Property Listings	+	+	Peak
Property Sales	–	–	Trough

Key

Peak = When a key driver is at its highest point, just before it begins to decline

Trough = When a key diver is at its lowest point, just before it begins to rise

+ = Increase in key driver

– = Decrease in key driver

ROI = Return on investment

(Refer to appendices for a list of all key driver peaks and troughs throughout a complete cycle.)

CHAPTER SUMMARY

- The slump is a difficult phase of the property cycle. Many inexperienced investors misunderstand the slump and believe that property prices will crash instantly when the market enters this phase.

- The beginning of the slump is characterised by slowly increasing vacancy rates due to an oversupply of rental accommodation, and subsequent decreasing returns from existing property investments in the form of reducing rents.

- By the middle of the slump, property is clearly out of favour as an investment vehicle. As people struggle financially under the pressure of diminished cashflow and decreasing or stalling values, forced sales of property become commonplace.

- The end of the slump is evidenced by several of the key drivers reaching troughs at around the same time. The property market lacks direction and property as an investment vehicle becomes noticeable by its absence from advisors' recommendations.

- At the beginning of the slump the prevailing motivating emotion is greed but by the end of the slump fear prevails.

Part 3

Investment Strategies Throughout the Property Cycle

Chapter 10

How to Survive the Property Cycle

While property values are cyclic, so too are many property investors. I have seen many people decide to invest in property near the end of the boom phase. Typically this occurs because they perceive that property is a sound investment purely because property values have risen over time. Unfortunately the fundamentals of a sound return on investment in the form of cashflow are often ignored because of these investors' expectations of potential short-term capital gains.

'Property investment is a marathon and not a sprint!'

There is a familiar pattern that inexperienced property investors seem to follow that I call . . .

The Six-Step Cycle to Slowly Going Broke by Investing in Property

Phase One: Realise that property investment has been a sound investment vehicle over the past few years. Attend a property seminar or read a property investment book or similar. Typically you already live in property you own and have some equity in it or have some cash available to invest.

Phase Two: Purchase first and then make subsequent property investments.

Phase Three: Property values move up by say 10%. Your equity increases and enables you to buy more property at higher prices. Purchase more property. Become hamstrung in your ability to finance further property purchases due to lack of equity and/or cashflow.

Phase Four: Property market crashes! Values drop by say 15%. Panic and rush to sell property due to a lack of cashflow, equity or both while values and rents are reducing. Incur real losses when selling your property investments.

Phase Five: Several years later the property market recovers strongly, with values up by say 15% or more.

Phase Six: Go back to Phase One!

Be Careful What You Wish For . . .

In New Zealand during the 1990s, many property investors had a common wish or goal to buy ten properties in ten years. These investors thought this would guarantee financial freedom, but by the time most investors had accumulated ten properties the property cycle had progressed into a slump. Property values and rents dropped and subsequently robbed them of their expected reward.

They soon realised that the number of properties was irrelevant when it came to defining financial freedom.

I have met many property investors who have expressed their dissatisfaction with property investment. I am staggered by the number of investors who have regretted buying one or more of the property investments in their portfolio. When I have asked why they bought the offending property in the first place, the replies have been much the same.

The answers have usually been something like, 'Because I didn't want to miss out on what appeared at the time to be a great investment opportunity,' or, 'The market was so buoyant I thought if I didn't hurry up and just buy any property that I would miss out on catching the wave of property value increases.'

To illustrate the point that the number of properties you own is irrelevant, consider the following case study of some clients whom I met in the year 2001.

WISH CASE STUDY

Wish

Commenced investing in property in March 1996 with a desire to purchase ten properties in the belief that this would ensure financial freedom.

Wish Granted?

By November 2001 they had accumulated the following property portfolio:

Number of properties	11
Total Value	$1,500,000
Total Mortgage	$1,200,000
Equity	$300,000
Cashflow (after tax rebates)	$17,000

Do you really think that the result achieved by November 2001 was the fulfilment of their wish? They had achieved their goal of ten properties, hadn't they? But the result after investing in property for over five years was certainly not the one initially anticipated. Their portfolio demanded that they spend a significant amount of time managing the tenants and maintaining the properties. If a property manager had been employed to take care of this, there would have been virtually no cashflow from the portfolio after expenses. These investors had no understanding that the property cycle even existed!

The funny thing is that I have seen several waves of increasing property values, and have learned that you don't need to catch them all. Instead if you are exceptionally fussy about which waves you decide to ride and when to catch them, you can actually have a relatively easy ride and achieve significant momentum with minimal resources.

So to reiterate: Be careful what you wish for, because you just might get it! If you are hoping for lots of property investments then you just might get them – but they may not deliver on the promise of financial freedom.

Many property investors simply try to accumulate as much property as they can in as short a time as possible, only to be disappointed with the end results. Worse still, some property investors find themselves overcommitted in relation to their financial or emotional resources and end up in the unenviable position of having to, or choosing to, sell down their property investments in times of financial hardship.

Financial Freedom or Financial Burden?

The overwhelming majority of property investors I have spoken to have told me that the number one reason they are investing in property is to achieve 'financial freedom'.

The problem is that when I ask them to define financial freedom, they typically hesitate and then tell me that financial freedom is having enough income to live on so they can effectively 'retire'. When I ask the next obvious question of how much income is enough, the response I usually get is, 'About what I am earning from my salary now.'

So if most property investors appear to have a goal of earning enough cashflow from their property investments to retire on, then why do so many of them buy property that delivers them little or negative cashflow?

> 'Most property investors focus on creating equity from property rather than creating cashflow.'

The downside of this approach is that you cannot retire on equity alone! You can however retire on adequate cashflow provided you *also* have adequate equity. While it is true that the more equity you have in your property portfolio, the more likely it is that you will enjoy a cashflow from your property investments, it is also true that most property investors enjoy little cashflow from their property.

I know thousands of property investors but only a handful who have achieved financial freedom through property. Clearly there are some fundamental differences between the 'average' property investors and the 'super successful' ones.

One of the most valuable qualities I have observed in successful property investors is their eagerness to walk away from every opportunity. Yes, I said eagerness to walk away! By training yourself to be a very reluctant purchaser, you will purchase only the very best opportunities you find.

Financial freedom is an elusive goal unless it can be clearly defined and placed in a timeframe within which it must be achieved. To make sure you actually achieve your desired outcome you will need to break down your goals into two distinct elements. Define your desired outcome in terms of these elements.

Because financial freedom consists of both elements, you need to make sure that every property purchase you make delivers adequate measures of each of these elements to take you closer to your goal.

> The two key elements of financial freedom for property investors:
>
> 1. Cashflow
>
> 2. Equity

It never ceases to amaze me how many novice property investors focus heavily on simply increasing the number of properties they own, rather than concentrating on what each property contributes to their overall return. Remember, the number of properties you accumulate has little bearing on whether you are a successful property investor. Your success or otherwise as a property investor will only ever be determined by the quality and the quantity of both your cashflow and your equity.

Adopt the Classic Traits of Successful Property Investors

A client who is one of the most successful investors I know was considering purchasing a piece of land with several building sites on which he would construct a number of properties for rental purposes. He did all his costings for materials and labour to complete the project, and calculated that he could have created over $500,000 in equity and a good cashflow. It would have taken him about 18 months to complete this project.

The amazing thing was that he walked away from this opportunity because he didn't believe it was good enough! I was curious about why he would walk away from such a fantastic deal. His response was that if he was going to work full-time on a project like this for 18 months then he wanted to make it worth his while!

He went on to find another opportunity that created him over $1 million in equity and an even stronger cashflow for less time and resources invested.

I have learned so many lessons from my most successful clients, and the best way for me to explain them is to outline their traits for you. The following list reveals the classic traits of the most successful property investors I have ever met. This list is by no means comprehensive but encompasses the main attributes I have observed after assessing thousands of property investors and their portfolios. They are almost always:

1. **Focused**
   They are alert to the influencing factors on the property market, the likely outcome of those factors and the opportunities they may present.

2. **Selective**
   They are exceptionally careful as to where, why and how they invest any of their resources. They understand that the cost of taking up any opportunity is that it uses up resources which could have been employed in pursuing an alternative opportunity. They come across as reluctant investors due to their selectiveness.

3. **Analytical**
   They leave nothing to chance. Everything is analysed from the perspectives of worst-case scenario and best-case scenario.

4. **Persistent**
   They never give up. They see every closed door as a positive step in a better direction and they seek opportunity in adversity.

5. **Goal oriented**
   They consistently set goals in writing, and regularly review them by measuring and managing their progress towards those goals.

6. **Conscientious**
   They will do whatever amount of work it takes to achieve their goals.

7. **Ambitious (but quietly)**
   They have big but realistic goals, but usually keep these to themselves.

8. **Personal growth seekers**

   They are committed to multi-dimensional growth (not just financial growth). They read a variety of self-improvement books to understand personal growth techniques.

9. **Passionate about property**

   They are thirsty for information, ideas, tools and other people's experiences in property.

10. **Determined (almost stubbornly) but patient**

    They possess an underlying determination and a patience strong enough to take any setbacks or delays their property investments may thrust upon them.

11. **Comfortable with calculated risks**

    They are not frightened by big numbers, but they always thoroughly research the potential risks before making a commitment. They understand and practise the wise words of Donald Trump when he said, 'Make sure you can survive the downside and the upside will take care of itself.'

12. **Looking for and actively courting change**

    They are continually looking for potential change both inside and outside their own control. They are proactive to either protect themselves from potential negative change or to instigate or capitalise on positive change.

13. **Open to considering new opportunities and ideas**

    They welcome the chance to consider new opportunities and ideas, but always complete their own due diligence to ensure they are fully aware of the risks before taking action.

14. **Flexible**

    They are prepared to consider changing strategies to achieve their goals.

The Successful Property Investor's Classic Traits Checklist

The following checklist may help to identify which of these success traits you already possess, and which you need.

	Got it	Need it
Focused		
I can focus on what I need to do to get the result I need.	_____	_____
Selective		
I am careful how I invest my limited resources.	_____	_____
Analytical		
When investing I leave nothing to chance, I always consider the worst-case scenario and make sure that I am prepared to live with it if it does eventuate.	_____	_____
Persistent		
I consider every closed door to be a positive opening for a better opportunity.	_____	_____
Goal oriented		
I am clear on what I want to achieve and have written goals which I regularly review.	_____	_____
Conscientious		
I will gladly do whatever amount of work is required to achieve my goals.	_____	_____
Ambitious		
I have big but realistic goals.	_____	_____
Personal growth seeker		
I am committed to multi-dimensional growth.	_____	_____
Passion		
I am thirsty for property investment knowledge.	_____	_____

(cont.)

	Got it	Need it
Determined but patient I possess enough determination to accept setbacks without giving up.	_____	_____
Comfortable with calculated risks I am not frightened of big numbers but always fully research my risks.	_____	_____
Embrace and actively court change I am continually seeking change because I know that's where opportunity lies.	_____	_____
Open to new ideas I welcome the chance to consider new opportunities and ideas.	_____	_____
Flexible I am prepared to consider changing strategies to achieve my goals.	_____	_____

Ride Out the Property Cycle

Property values increase and decrease at specific times during the property cycle, but ultimately values have a long-term positive trend based on the simple law of supply and demand. Given enough time,

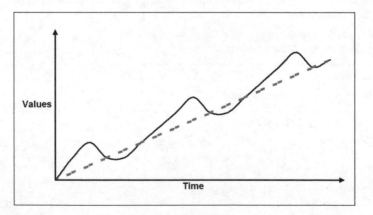

Graph 10.1

property values oscillate between exceeding this long-term positive trend during a boom and falling short of it during a slump (see Graph 10.1).

An example of my own experience with oscillating property values is the house I purchased in 1989 for $95,000. In 1992 (during the property cycle's slump phase) I had the same house revalued to find it had a value of only $70,000! Fortunately I understood that in time the value would rebound.

In 1994 (during the property cycle's recovery phase) I again had the house valued to find it was worth $120,000 and then in 1995 it was valued at $140,000 and in 1996 (during the property cycle's boom phase) at $160,000. I sold the house in 1997 (as the property cycle entered the slump phase) for $189,000.

I could have sold this house in 1992 and I would have realised a loss of $25,000 but instead I made $94,000 and I learned the wisdom of riding out the property cycle rather than selling in a slump and taking a loss.

Property Investment Risk Management

The risk factor of property investment is significant. Yes, it's true, you will increase your risk profile as a result of investing in property but the rewards to be enjoyed can be significant with little cash input. The risk profile you are comfortable with will pretty much determine how aggressive or passive your property investment activities are.

As a general rule of thumb the higher your risk profile, the higher your risk will be but also the higher your rewards should be.

So how are you going to have a stress-free sleep at night when you owe the bank hundreds of thousands or even millions of dollars? Easy, you just need to focus on minimising your risks and ensuring you always generate a positive cashflow from your property investments. Always remember that as a property investor your cashflow is your lifeblood. Without it you may well suffer financial stress.

If you are at the front end of the baby boomer population (born around 1946–52) and are now considering property investment as a vehicle to create wealth, it's probably not the time for you to be too aggressive with your investment in property as you can't afford a high-risk exposure at this stage. However, if you are near the tail end of baby boomers (born 1958–61) and are considering property investment, then you may suit a more aggressive profile.

If you were born before 1946 and are just now considering property investment, you will most likely need a very conservative exposure, as at this stage in your life it is not wise to take a high-risk approach to investment.

> 'Irrespective of their age, the most successful property investors I have met have been long-term investors.'

Successful investors make plans to ensure they can afford to hold their property portfolio over the long term. They are thus able to ride out the ups and downs of the property cycle.

To hold on to a property portfolio you will typically need the following attributes:

Prudent Borrowing Levels

This is dependent on your financial resources – how much income and equity you have access to – as well as your risk profile. Unless you are prepared to take big risks, be careful of over-gearing (borrowing 90% or more of your property's value) because in the event that values decrease, your financier may insist on a lump-sum reduction of your mortgage to reduce their own risk. If you are then not in a position to make such a reduction to satisfy your financier, you may be forced to sell some or all of your property. This can obviously prove disastrous for your financial position.

Regular Maintenance Programme

A schedule of regular maintenance undertaken to ensure that the optimum rental income can be achieved is sensible.

Being Proactive with Tenants

Be alert to the requirements of tenants to ensure stability of tenancy. This can include reducing rents (before your tenant indicates they have found cheaper accommodation) when overall rental levels are decreasing. Or if you are reluctant to reduce rents, tell your tenants you wish to upgrade the building and ask them what they would prefer done. They are less likely to vacate your building for a cheaper alternative if you have upgraded it to their liking.

Access to Adequate Credit Facilities or Cash

Make sure you have access to sources of finance that are not reliant on the value of your property portfolio. In the event that values decline, you should still be able to access finance for repairs and maintenance and to cover any vacancies your property may experience. To be safe you should first calculate your total fixed outgoings for three months. By total fixed outgoings I mean the cost of *everything* you need – all mortgages, rates, insurances, and living expenses such as food, petrol, etc. Now assume you will receive no income from any source for three months. If you do not have access to sufficient funds to cover all your outgoings for at least that period with no income at all, then you do not have access to adequate credit facilities or cash.

Interest Rate Risk Management Strategy

Even professional economists are not always able to predict events that can significantly influence interest rates. So how do you reduce the impact of big upward swings in mortgage interest rates as well as get some benefit if interest rates decrease?

When I researched this question in 1997 I found very little information available on how I could protect my interest cost exposure as a borrower. But what I did understand was how to protect myself as an investor in shares – for example by using a strategy called Dollar Cost Averaging which is commonly employed to minimise investment risk when investing in shares.

If Dollar Cost Averaging was a valid risk minimisation strategy for investing, I considered how I could apply the same theory to borrowing. So I thought to myself: Maybe I could use a similar concept to minimise my interest rate risk. This gave rise to the concept of Interest Rate Averaging.

Dollar Cost Averaging is an investment strategy whereby you invest a fixed dollar amount on a regular basis, usually monthly, to purchase shares or shares in a mutual fund. If the share price declines at one of these regular intervals when your fixed dollar investment is made, you receive slightly more shares for the same fixed investment amount, and if the share price is up you receive slightly fewer shares. This simply minimises your risk of buying all the shares at peak levels as they are not all purchased at the same time.

Interest Rate Averaging is a method that many property investors now utilise as an effective interest rate risk management strategy. Interest Rate Averaging is achieved by splitting mortgage debt into several smaller loans and then taking different interest rate terms on each loan.

For example, if you have a $600,000 mortgage you can split this amount into six separate $100,000 loans and take differing interest rate terms on each loan.

Loan 1	$100,000	Variable (Floating)
Loan 2	$100,000	Fixed for 1 year
Loan 3	$100,000	Fixed for 2 years
Loan 4	$100,000	Fixed for 3 years
Loan 5	$100,000	Fixed for 4 years
Loan 6	$100,000	Fixed for 5 years

This means you have an averaged interest rate on your total borrowings; if interest rates increase by say 3% p.a. your averaged interest rate on total borrowings will only increase by 0.5% p.a.!

At the end of each twelve-month period, $100,000 of debt will expire from its fixed interest rate. So each year you will only need to decide whether to float or fix that $100,000. This is a much more manageable decision to make than whether to fix or float the total loan amount.

Interest rates will continue to be volatile in the long term, so is it worth risking a lifetime of investing by not having a strategy to minimise your interest rate risk? Many people opt for a variable interest rate (when short-term interest rates are low), and sometimes will incur early repayment penalties of several thousands of dollars to break fixed rates so they can enjoy a lower short-term rate. Their intention is usually to watch interest rate levels and take a fixed rate if rates start to increase. This appears to be a somewhat short-term solution to a long-term (mortgage) commitment.

For example, if interest rates start to increase and we take a fixed rate, we may find a few months later that rates are back down or, worse still, considerably lower than when we (wisely) decided to fix the rate!

Interest Rate Averaging offers many advantages including:

- Less interest rate risk.

- Less stress when making a decision on whether to fix or float.

- The opportunity to gain some of the benefit of reducing rates (a portion of our debt will be on a floating rate, so if floating rates decrease so does our overall interest cost).

The downside of Interest Rate Averaging is that each time we take a fixed rate a bank redocumentation fee may apply due to redisclosure requirements. This fee obviously affects our costs (and effectively increases our true interest rate), but the benefits of Interest Rate Averaging should outweigh this cost.

Interest Rate Averaging is not perfect science, but it goes a long way to relieving the difficult decision of whether to fix or float our mortgage.

Avoiding the One-Bank Trap

Many property investors are unable to make a property purchase when offered an exceptional opportunity because their existing financier is already either comfortable with their exposure or uncomfortable with their proposed exposure, so they decline the request. This is the same financier that consistently agreed to help you buy an existing property portfolio!

The advantages of having several financier relationships far outweigh those of having just one.

By using more than one financier you can achieve:

1. The ability to have a choice of products that suit your specific circumstances rather than take the potentially inflexible offer of one lender.

2. The luck to be with the right bank when one of them decides to loosen up on their criteria to attract more business from property investors.

3. The ability to negotiate with more than one lender for the best price and the best finance.

4. The ability to approach a loan request laterally.

Sometimes lateral thinking is required on your part to achieve your end result of raising finance for an additional property purchase.

If you find one or more of your financiers believe you will be over-committing yourself financially by making additional purchases, some simple restructuring may be in order. Such restructuring may include placing some debt on an interest-only basis, rather than a principal-and-interest basis, and/or reducing any other fixed monthly commitments you may have. Hire purchase lending, for example, has a significant negative impact on your borrowing capacity and can mean the difference between getting an approval for additional borrowing or a refusal. It may pay to refinance hire purchase borrowings over a longer term to reduce your monthly commitments. Seek advice from a competent mortgage broker who has significant experience dealing with property investors, as they will most likely understand your needs.

A good example of a simple restructuring was a client of my New Zealand mortgage broking company. This client had the opportunity to buy an adjacent property to one he already owned.

Buying the neighbouring property would not only enable access to the rear of his existing property, resulting in the ability to subdivide it into two sites, but it would also allow the creation of an additional site by subdividing the neighbouring site too. The potential value to be unlocked by subdividing was significant as it effectively created two new sites. My client's intention was to build two additional rental properties on the two new sites.

His existing bank declined his request for finance to buy the neighbouring property, claiming that he would be overcommitted financially. He sought our advice and we found that his principal payments per month were so large that they restricted his borrowing capacity. By restructuring his mortgages to an interest-only basis (with his existing lender, who agreed to this request) and introducing another bank to fund the new purchase, we were able to achieve his goal of buying the neighbouring site and creating significant value by subdividing and building two additional rental properties.

The opportunity nearly did not eventuate because of his initial reliance on only one bank to build his portfolio.

I have never seen a detrimental result from having several financier relationships but I have often seen it with clients who have chosen to be loyal to just one financier. You need to maintain control of your own destiny, and if you have everything with one financier you have effectively put all your eggs in one basket! You may find that your goals are being restricted by a financier focusing on their own goals – usually to have a limited exposure to as many different clients as possible!

Protection from Loss of Income Through Disability

In the event you become disabled or your main source of income suffers for some reason, you don't want to find yourself in the position of having to sell down your property portfolio to raise cash. Consider taking out some form of insurance to protect your income from these events.

Legislative Changes

Stay informed about the potential impacts that changing legislation can have on your property portfolio. Make sure you have access to professional advisors who can inform you of any proposed changes that may affect you. You can also subscribe to relevant publications which will keep you up to date on changes in the property industry.

Loss of Rental Income

Consider protecting the lifeblood of your ability to finance your property portfolio. Just as you can protect your personal income from loss with suitable insurance, you can protect your rental income through various forms of rent insurance.

Mortality

Again, consider protecting your loved ones from financial hardship or loss in the event you unexpectedly leave this mortal coil. Life insurance is readily available in many forms, which can include instant lump-sum payments to named beneficiaries and/or an ongoing annuity. Make sure you have a written and up-to-date will to ensure there is no confusion for the potential beneficiaries you will leave behind.

Property Investment Risk Management Checklist

The following checklist may help to identify which of these risk management systems you already possess and which you should consider addressing.

	Yes	No
Prudent borrowing levels		
My borrowing level matches my risk profile.	_____	_____
Regular maintenance programme		
I have a regular property maintenance programme in place.	_____	_____
Being proactive with tenants		
I have a system for dealing proactively with my tenants.	_____	_____
Access to adequate credit facilities or cash		
I have access to enough credit facilities.	_____	_____
Interest rate risk management strategy		
My interest rate exposure is minimised.	_____	_____
Avoiding the one-bank trap		
I have several financiers funding the growth of my portfolio.	_____	_____
Legislative changes		
I keep informed of potential legislative changes.	_____	_____
Loss of income		
I have protected my sources of income.	_____	_____
Mortality		
I have protected my loved ones in the event of my departure.	_____	_____

CHAPTER SUMMARY

- Remember that property investment is a marathon and not a sprint.

- Many people decide (wrongly) to invest in property near the end of the boom phase.

- Unfortunately the principle of a sound return on investment in the form of cashflow is often ignored in the anticipation of potential capital gains.

- Don't fall into the trap of slowly going broke by investing in property when the market is in the boom phase and then selling in the slump phase.

- Financial freedom is an elusive goal unless it can be clearly defined and placed in a timeframe within which it must be achieved.

- Remember the number of properties you accumulate has little bearing on whether you are a successful property investor.

- Adopt the classic traits of successful property investors.

- Successful investors make plans to ensure they can afford to hold their property portfolio over the long term.

- Put in place effective risk management systems.

Chapter 11

When is it a Good Time to Buy Property?

As I mentioned at the beginning of this book the one question I have been asked over and over again, irrespective of whether property prices are increasing, decreasing or stable, is this: 'Is now the right time to invest in property?'

Some people believe there are only specific times in the property cycle when you should buy property and other times when you should not buy any property at all. There certainly are some optimum times in the property cycle to be buying, such as at the end of the slump and the beginning of the recovery phase. But I am of the firm opinion that it is always a good time to buy a good deal and a good deal is what I refer to as a SAFE deal.

The acronym **SAFE** stands for:

S = Sensible based on your specific financial circumstances

A sensible property is one that offers a positive cashflow, assuming the full purchase price is borrowed at the outset and the positive cashflow is prior to any tax rebates. These circumstances are ideally combined with sound long-term capital growth prospects. While there are genuine exceptions to this fundamental rule of investing, they only arise in specific circumstances. For example, I know many property investors who generate extremely strong cashflows from a combination of business and property investments, who choose to purchase property that delivers a negative cashflow. However they will only do so if they can achieve a purchase price that reflects a significant discount on the current valuation. This may arise where property is situated in superior locations, or where buildings on the property require significant renovation and there is an opportunity to create a strong increase in value as a result of such renovations. So for property investors with extremely strong cashflows it can still sometimes be sensible to buy negatively geared property.

A = Affordable so the property is not likely to become financially overwhelming

If for example a 3% interest rate rise will make your mortgage repayments unaffordable and will result in you having to sell the property, then the property is not affordable for you.

F = Friendly vendor

A vendor who is keener to sell than you are to buy. Friendly vendors will sell at a value that makes the purchase a good buy for you irrespective of the property cycle.

E = Easily rentable or resellable

Avoid unusual properties which could prove hard to rent or resell (i.e. boarding houses, or buildings with structural problems).

Smart investors always make sure they can survive the potential downsides of every property purchase if unexpected circumstances arise that may adversely affect values.

At any given time there are always two distinct property markets for buyers. Here is a definition of these two markets.

The Emotional Property Market

This is the market in which most people buy their family home. The buying decision (and the selling decision from the vendor) is driven more by emotion than logic. The purchase price and/or terms are determined mainly by the vendor as they are under little or no pressure to sell but, by contrast, you are under an emotional pressure to buy. If you buy investment property in this market you are what I refer to as a desperate purchaser. Unfortunately I have seen many investors purchase property on emotion alone while being convinced the buying decision was a logical one! Such emotions often include the fear, combined with greed, of missing out on potential capital growth.

Property can be very emotional but you must resist this influencing your purchasing decision. If you allow yourself to become emotionally attached to property you may make an irrational purchasing decision. Remember that property just happens to be one of your chosen investment vehicles. When you invest in other asset classes such as shares or bonds they don't exert an emotional influence on your choice, do they?

You should treat property investment in exactly the same way.

> "Make sure you are more emotionally attached to the money you are about to invest in the property than you are to the actual building/s you are buying.'

Even if you are borrowing most or all of the funds to make the property purchase, you should still have the same unemotional approach to the building/s you are investing in.

If you fear that you may be letting emotion influence any investment decision, you should seek a second opinion from someone who has experience with such investments.

The Investor Property Market

This is the market in which you should buy your investment property (in the main) if you want to maximise the results of your investment. The vendor will typically be either very keen to sell or will have little choice but to sell. Your buying decision is driven more by logic than emotion because the numbers need to be right – otherwise you will not buy. The vendor's selling decision is driven by external factors such as creditors or a bank, or some other reason that holds more importance than necessarily achieving a fair market value.

As a general rule the logic for determining an acceptable purchase price is to ensure you achieve a surplus cashflow from the proposed rental income after all cash expenses. (If the cashflow achieves a surplus only as a result of a tax refund, then generally you are paying too much to buy the property as a long-term rental investment.)

Some inexperienced investors will happily buy property that has a negative surplus cashflow based on the belief (or hope) that the property will deliver superior capital growth. As mentioned earlier in this chapter this strategy can suit high income earners, but it does not suit the large majority of investors due to its heavy reliance on other sources of income to make such an investment viable in the short to medium term.

Here is an example of achieving a positive cashflow prior to any tax rebate:

Income
Rent $300/week x 52 weeks p.a.   **$15,600**

Less Expenses
Mortgage Interest (assumes 100%
of purchase price is borrowed) $12,000
Council Rates/Levies $1,200
Insurance (Fire/Earthquake) $400
Repairs & Maintenance $1,000
Subtotal   −$14,600

Surplus Cashflow
(this figure needs to be positive)   **$1,000**

Plus Taxation Advantage
Tax Refund   +$1,500

Total Cashflow   **$2,500**

When you buy in the investor market the purchase price and terms are determined mainly by you, since you are under little or no pressure to buy; the vendor on the other hand has little or no choice but to sell. The vendor is therefore what I refer to as a desperate or keen vendor.

One problem with trying to find a keen vendor is that they are not always easy to recognise. Put yourself in the shoes of a desperate vendor. You need to sell your property quickly as you have little choice. Are you likely to contact your local real estate agent and tell them, 'I must sell now!' Somehow I doubt it. You are more likely to indicate that you are keen to sell but of course not so keen to accept any old offer or an offer representing a heavy discount on your perception of the current market value.

So how do you as a prospective purchaser identify a desperate vendor? Sometimes you need to be something of a Sherlock Holmes in order to piece together clues. I personally experienced such an occasion a few years ago when I was considering making an offer to purchase a house converted into multiple properties as an investment. At the time the local property cycle had been experiencing a slump for the preceding four years, and this house was located in a superior location on the city fringe of Auckland. I knew the recovery phase was imminent so I was considering purchases in quality and city fringe locations (refer to the wise investor's property strategies later in this chapter).

I asked the real estate agent the same question I always ask when considering any property purchase: 'Why is this vendor selling?'

The agent informed me that the vendors were a married couple who had no specific reason for selling. That was the first, elementary clue for me that the vendor might be keen. I have never met anyone who was selling their property for no specific reason. When you think about it, there is always some reason for selling. The vendors either have something else they *want* to do with the money or something else they *have* to do with the money. Either way there is always a reason for selling and if they, or their agent, are not willing to disclose this reason then there is every likelihood they don't want you to know because it indicates how keen they are to sell!

The agent then informed me that the vendors occupied one of the dwellings in the house, so I paid special attention to that one. The second clue I gleaned after viewing several of the rooms occupied by the owners and I realised that no less than four of them had wedding photos displayed even though they had been married for several years. This raised my suspicion that the vendors might be overcompensating to hide a marital split that necessitated their selling the property. The agent continued to show me round and I was delighted to find a large walk-in wardrobe off the master bedroom. I was equally delighted to find my third elementary clue to the vendors' circumstances when I walked inside this wardrobe. I noticed that there were only three pairs of women's shoes in the wardrobe and I figured that the woman vendor was probably wearing a further pair as she was not on site, so that meant that she only had four pairs of shoes. Now, I don't believe I have ever met a woman with just four pairs of shoes. I suspected she may no longer be residing with her husband.

My deduction based on these clues was that there was a strong likelihood this married couple were parting ways, and hence the imminent sale of this property. I asked the agent whether this was the case but he denied it. Perhaps he wasn't aware of the vendors' circumstances, or didn't want to be aware of them.

In any event I did purchase this property for a good price – at a discount from the independent valuation I obtained. Taking account of the purchase price and my rental assessments for the multiple properties at the time, the house also met my criterion of delivering a positive cashflow before any tax rebate.

Interestingly enough I found out after my purchase of this property that the vendors had actually separated and the woman vendor had not occupied the house for some time. Of course I was not surprised because I already suspected that was the case.

To find a keen or desperate vendor you do need to be observant and seek out the subtle and the not-so-subtle clues. The more clues you can find, the more likely you are to be able to fill in the missing pieces and ascertain whether or not you are dealing with a keen vendor.

Sometimes you will find keen vendors easily because they will be selling their property privately (to avoid real estate agents' fees) or even at auction or a mortgagee sale where the sale is being forced by a financier. Vendors can become more desperate over time, so it also pays to consider property that has been listed with real estate agents for a while.

> **'Don't waste your time with an unmotivated vendor.'**

There are however exceptions to this rule. A friend of mine, Tom, recently purchased a property situated next door to two properties he already owned. The vendor was stubborn and insisted on selling at the market value as appraised by a valuer.

The reason Tom could still buy this property in the investor property market was because it made sense from an investment perspective to him. It simply would not have made sense as an investment for anyone else at the price he paid.

The reasons it made sense to Tom were:

1. He could transfer some of the land from the property he bought to his own neighbouring property, allowing an additional property to be built on the site.

2. He increased the market value of his other neighbouring property by the addition of an outdoor living area on some of the land formerly owned by the neighbour.

3. The newly acquired site was of a sufficient size even after the transfer of some of the land to the neighbouring properties to enable an additional property to be built.

The net result to him was much greater than the fact he had to pay market value for the property.

The Wise Investor's Property Cycle Strategies

In every phase of the property cycle there are specific investing strategies employed by wise property investors.

The key to all of these strategies is that they result in ownership of property which generally delivers a positive cashflow.

You may not be in a financial position to take advantage of some of these purchasing strategies throughout the entire property cycle. However you will note that I have identified whether the key focus for each phase is to increase cashflow, or equity, or both.

> 'If you focus on employing specific strategies that can strengthen any weaknesses in your financial position, whether it be equity or cashflow, you will be better placed to take advantage of subsequent property cycles.'

For example, if you need to create equity then you can position yourself to benefit from equity growth during the boom by purchasing in quality locations, especially if you purchase a do-up or renovation opportunity, at the beginning of the recovery.

The table opposite reveals which strategies wise investors employ, when and why.

RECOVERY

The key focus during the recovery phase is to increase cashflow and to position yourself to benefit from equity growth in the coming boom.

Beginning

Purchase property and do-ups in quality and upper socio-economic locations and CBD fringe.

Middle

Purchase property and do-ups in quality and upper socio-economic locations. Accumulate land in the best quality locations suitable for building, for the purpose of creating positive cashflow.

End

Purchase property and do-ups in mid-socio-economic locations. Accumulate land in the best mid-socio-economic locations where you can build and still achieve a positive cashflow.

BOOM

The key focus during the boom phase is to increase cashflow and maximise equity creation.

Beginning

Purchase property in lower to mid-socio-economic locations. Build on any already owned vacant land.

Middle and End

Implement strategies to generate additional cashflow from existing or newly acquired property.

End

Implement strategies to generate additional cashflow from existing or newly acquired property. Sell property that has not performed well, carries too much downside risk or has significant ongoing maintenance costs which affect the long-term financial viability of the property. Possibly also sell property to free up cash for diversification into other investment vehicles or to fund lifestyle choices.

SLUMP

The key focus during the slump phase is to increase cashflow.

Beginning
Purchase newly constructed property in forced sale situations (for example mortgagee sales) to secure positive cashflow.

Middle
Purchase property in mid-socio-economic areas from forced sale situations or keen vendors exiting the property market.

End
Purchase quality property and do-ups with character or charm in quality and upper socio-economic locations and CBD fringe, to position yourself for strong equity growth.

CHAPTER SUMMARY

- It is always the right time to buy a good deal, and a good deal is a SAFE deal.

  S = Sensible
  A = Affordable
  F = Friendly vendor
  E = Easily rentable

- At any given time there are always two distinct property markets you can buy in: emotional and investor.

- The *emotional property market* is the market in which most people buy their family home. If you buy investment property in this market you are what I refer to as a desperate purchaser.

- When you buy in the emotional market the purchase price and/or terms are determined mainly by the vendor, as they are under little or no pressure to sell but by contrast you are under an emotional pressure to buy.

- The *investor property market* is the market from which you should buy your investment property (in the main). The logic that should determine an acceptable purchase price is to ensure you achieve a surplus cashflow.

- When you buy in the investor market the purchase price and terms are determined mainly by you, as the purchaser, since you are under little or no pressure to buy.

- In every phase of the property cycle wise property investors will typically employ specific investment strategies.

PART 4

Cycles
Within Cycles

Chapter 12

Finance and the Property Cycle

Finance plays a key role in the property cycle, and financiers' willingness to lend on property varies depending on what phase the property cycle is experiencing. There are times when obtaining finance for property purchases is incredibly easy and other times when it is extremely difficult. Once you understand how inextricably linked the property cycle and finance are, you will realise why financiers seem to be fair-weather friends when it comes to their readiness or otherwise to lend for investment property purchases.

Finance is linked to the property cycle in two ways: first, by the *finance availability cycle* which determines the ease of obtaining finance to fund property purchases; and second, by the *cycle of losses* which reflects financiers' levels of losses. Both of these cycles are in synchronisation with the property cycle.

'The careful path financiers must follow to make profits from lending on property is fraught with danger because of the property cycle's significant influence on their lending exposure levels.'

Property is often highly leveraged by borrowers, so a small decrease in values can significantly increase a financier's exposure to potential losses. This is why there is a time for financiers to lend aggressively on property but there is also a time for them to exercise caution when lending.

The Finance Availability Cycle

The finance availability cycle reflects the fact that most property investors' borrowing capacity is adversely affected during the slump due to reduced levels of rents and possibly values. Also, financiers' lending policies are adjusted throughout the property cycle to either reduce their risk or increase their lending exposure to property.

For example, at the end of a slump phase financiers will typically ease up on their lending policy and make financing property purchases easier than during the beginning and middle of the slump phase. This enables financiers to increase their exposure to the

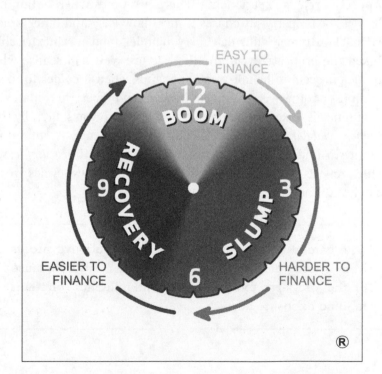

property sector at the end of a slump, as the risk premium of lending on property is considered to be low at this point.

Conversely, at the end of the boom and beginning of the slump the risk premium for lending on property will increase in the opinion of the financiers so they will typically tighten their lending policy to reduce their exposure to the property sector. This in turn adversely affects property borrowers' ability to fund additional property purchases and therefore further reduces the demand for property.

The Cycle of Losses

Financiers tend to have periods where they experience very few losses and other times when many losses are incurred.

This cycle of losses typically follows the progression of the property cycle because such a large amount of finance raised is to fund property assets. Property is globally the single largest physical asset class, so borrowing for property represents a large proportion of

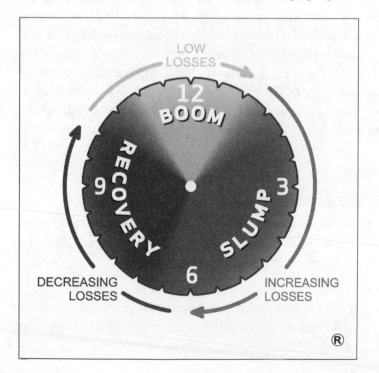

a financier's lending exposure. It is only common sense that the cycle of losses will follow the property cycle. As the property cycle progresses into the slump and property values stall or decline, the financiers' losses start to increase as they struggle to recoup some of their lending secured by property. The financiers suffer as a result of many borrowers defaulting on their repayment obligations. This in turn leads to mortgagee sales by the financiers and ultimately results in losses being incurred. These losses can potentially bankrupt a financier.

New Zealand's cycle of losses in the early 1990s severely impacted on the financial well-being of the former state-owned bank called the Bank of New Zealand (BNZ). At the time the BNZ suffered huge losses which were primarily a result of business and investment lending, including property investment lending, and subsequently required a huge cash injection from the government of hundreds of millions of taxpayer dollars.

Just a short time later the BNZ was sold as part of the government's asset sale programme to divest itself of commercial enterprise. This sale was made at the worst possible time from the perspective of the cycle of losses, because it was the end of the loss phase of the cycle and the majority of losses had already been incurred before the sale was made. This was evidenced in the following years as the BNZ reported good profits for their new owners.

CHAPTER SUMMARY

- The *finance availability cycle* reflects the fact that financiers' lending policies are adjusted throughout the property cycle to either reduce risk or increase exposure.

- The *cycle of losses* reflects the fact that financiers tend to have cyclical periods of experiencing very few losses and other times where many losses are incurred.

Chapter 13

The End of the Property Cycle?

There has been much international commentary in the last few years about house price growth outstripping rental increases, and the fact that property returns (rental incomes in relation to property values) are now significantly lower than they have been in the past. Such commentary suggests that house prices are too high in light of the low financial returns currently being achieved. The point is also made that any investment in residential property will be detrimentally affected if interest rates return to the 10% levels seen in the early to mid-1990s. However, little comment has been made about the fact that many countries' government-controlled Reserve Banks now have inflationary restraints maintained by strict economic policy targets. These targets effectively create a more controlled inflation environment resulting in less need to hike interest rates to curb rampant inflation, as occurred in the 1980s. Internationally in 2004 we have lower interest rates than we have seen for several decades.

Interest rates certainly can increase rapidly, and if international interest rates increased most countries would have little option but to follow that trend. However wise property investors would view this only as an opportune time to accumulate more sound property investments. Of course wise investors will have an interest rate risk management strategy in place (such as interest rate averaging, as outlined in Chapter 10), to protect their own cashflow from any sharp interest rate rises and position themselves to be able to accumulate more property.

Ironically, when interest rates do rise rapidly the opportunity to purchase positive cashflow property often quickly becomes apparent. This is because when interest rates rise, most property investors have a reduced borrowing capacity. Some will even experience financial duress and need to dispose of property at values which can provide the new owner with a positive cashflow.

Typically, few investors will be able, or prepared, to increase their own risk and take on new debt at the higher interest rates. Therefore the few property investors actively in the market at this time can insist on buying only property that will result in a positive cashflow after accounting for the higher interest rates. The opportune time to buy is actually created by higher interest rates at a time when most others can't, or won't, buy.

Lower yields from residential property investment are now being accepted internationally. While interest rates remain low, and to some extent are controlled via inflationary control measures, lower yields will be acceptable to property investors. Of course in the event that interest rates increase significantly, higher yields will be insisted upon and property values may well suffer – although this would not

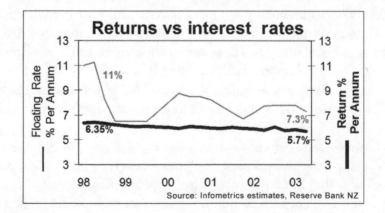

Graph 13.1

result in the end of the property cycle. After all, interest rates are merely a market influencer (refer to Chapter 6).

The Baby Boomer Impact

There has been some commentary about the ever-ageing population of baby boomers (born between 1946–61) and the impact they could have on asset prices as they all reach retirement age and cash up their investment assets over the next twenty years or so. This will most likely have some effect on the supply-and-demand equation of property from about the year 2006, and possibly up until the year 2021. The point made is that the baby boomers will all want to realise their investment assets (such as property investments) during this timeframe so there will be a baby boomer property crash – an oversupply of property on the market and not enough demand to ensure property holds its value.

'We are unlikely to witness a baby boomer-induced property crash caused by a mass exodus from property.'

This is because property is an income-generating asset, and many retirees will simply rely on the income from renting out their property rather than selling it at a reduced value. It is doubtful whether there will in fact be a baby boomer property crash because the finance industry will eagerly satisfy the baby boomers' need to realise cash from their properties without actually having to sell them.

There are already reverse annuity mortgage products available which allow retirees to tap into their equity in property without the need to actually sell it. These products enable a property owner to be given a lump sum and sometimes an ongoing annuity for the rest of their lives, with ownership of the property reverting to the lender upon the owner passing away.

There will also be other creative financing solutions specifically designed to enable retirees to release the equity they have in property without the need to sell it at low values; in fact we can expect a plethora of such products to become available through mainstream lenders, who will eagerly satisfy the demand for financing solutions as the baby boomers reach retirement age. What we are likely to see is an orderly adjustment to the supply levels of new properties instead of a sudden downward correction in property values.

Common Objections to the Concept of the Property Cycle

It is actually good news that many people either refuse to acknowledge the property cycle actually exists or, even if they accept it has existed in the past, believe it will not do so in the future. Here is a list of common objections raised by those who refute the concept of the property cycle, and the logical answers to these objections.

1. Property market forces are random (the forces that are perceived to create property cycles are random therefore cannot be forecast).

   The property market forces or key drivers' historical trends can be modelled against the house price index to determine their collective historical patterns in relation to former property cycles. These key drivers can then collectively be used to assess the likely short-term impacts on the house price index.

2. Cycles cannot be consistently measured (even if there is a property cycle it is impossible to measure it, or to determine where the property market is in relation to the cycle).

   The majority of the key drivers can be consistently measured giving a good insight into the most likely progression of the property cycle in the near future.

3. No one can consistently predict market trends accurately so cycles cannot be forecast (there is no such thing as a crystal ball). The argument is that even if there is a property cycle and even if it can be measured, any historical data or pattern

cannot be used to forecast what the property cycle will do in the future.

History does not necessarily repeat but the chance of repetition of an outcome is increased when the same forces that previously resulted in a certain outcome are at play.

4. If property cycles haven't been studied in great depth before to predict their pattern and likely future pattern, then why should they be studied now? (If it hasn't already been discovered it mustn't exist.)

At one time the world was believed to be flat too. It has been said that the only way to find the limits of the possible is to venture into the impossible.

5. If someone understood the property cycle and how to use it to their advantage why would they want the world to know about it? (Do they have their own agenda or their own interests at heart from sharing their knowledge?)

I cannot speak for others who have studied property cycles, but one of the motivations I have to present the findings of my research is to help as many other investors as I can so they can minimise their risks of investing in property. I have seen far too many investors suffer financially and emotionally from a lack of understanding of the basic concept of property cycles, while I have seen many others benefit from understanding the big-picture concept of property cycles. Of course there are also some benefits for my businesses (such as increased profile) as a result of sharing my knowledge.

6. Inadequate data exists to formulate a proper analysis (no concrete conclusions can be made as not enough data is available for all of the variables that influence the property market).

The majority of the key drivers have accurate records kept by local government statistics departments or economists.

7. The buy-and-hold strategy eliminates the need to have any understanding of the property cycle (it doesn't matter when

property is bought during a property cycle if it is held long term).

The buy-and-hold strategy does minimise the impact of what type of property you buy and when you buy it, but you can achieve so much more if you have even a basic understanding of the property cycle and which strategies to employ at various times in the cycle. I have met many property investors who have had to hold property for over seven years before the property was worth even what they had paid for it, simply because they naively bought property purely for expected capital gains at the end of a property boom.

Why the Property Cycle is Here to Stay

The question of whether property cycles will continue or whether they have had their day will no doubt be the topic of much discussion for another hundred years. Even Homer Hoyt questioned whether property cycles may be a passing phase in the final chapter of *100 Years of Land Values in Chicago*, written in 1933.

He finished his book by saying that the property cycle may be a passing phenomenon confined to rapidly growing cities. He also stated that property cycles are long and uncertain, therefore practical application of any of the precepts in his book could be difficult. His concern was that a boom seemed to occur only every twenty or thirty years so it would be difficult to take advantage of it. But evidence today indicates property cycles are shorter than they used to be. Perhaps we have more mature and therefore more efficient property markets which minimises the volatility of property cycles.

We all know that history does not necessarily accurately reflect the future, so how do we know that the property cycle will continue in its present form? The short answer is that while we don't know for sure, we do know that the property cycle has historically been shown to experience the three phases of recovery, boom and slump. We also know that this cycle exists as a result of the key drivers having consistent patterns culminating in peaks and troughs. These key drivers ultimately influence the levels of supply and demand which in turn influence the property market.

Unfortunately the time that it takes for the property cycle to complete its full course is not always consistent, and this too may throw some doubt on whether the property cycle will actually continue.

> 'It is no coincidence that some of Homer Hoyt's basic observations made over seventy years ago have withstood the test of time.'

Based on my own observations of the three phases of recovery, boom and slump, combined with the analysis I have made of the key drivers, I am of the firm opinion that we can expect the property cycle to last at least another seventy years. As long as supply and demand are allowed to determine the value of property, I believe the property cycle will prevail.

CHAPTER SUMMARY

- Lower interest rates have led to the acceptance of lower property yields.

- Ironically when interest rates do rise rapidly the opportunity to purchase positive cashflow property quickly becomes apparent.

- A baby boomer property crash is unlikely because the finance industry will eagerly satisfy the baby boomers' need to realise cash from their properties without actually having to sell them.

- Many common but unfounded objections exist to the concept of the property cycle, and there are logical answers to such objections.

- The historical property cycle has been shown to generally experience the three phases of recovery, boom and slump.

- We can expect the property cycle pattern to last at least another seventy years.

- As long as supply and demand are allowed to determine the value of property, the property cycle will prevail.

Appendices

Government Economic Data Websites

AUSTRALIA

http://www.aph.gov.au/library/intguide/STATS/ecindicators.htm
http://wopared.parl.net/library/pubs/mesi/

Australian Bureau of Statistics

http://www.abs.gov.au

NEW ZEALAND
Statistics New Zealand

http://www.stats.govt.nz/

UK
National Statistics On Line

http://www.statistics.gov.uk

USA

http://www.whitehouse.gov/fsbr/esbr.html
http://www.economicindicators.gov/

US Census Bureau

http://factfinder.census.gov

SOUTH AFRICA

http://www.absa.co.za/absa_library (click on Economic Research)

Property Cycle Peaks and Troughs

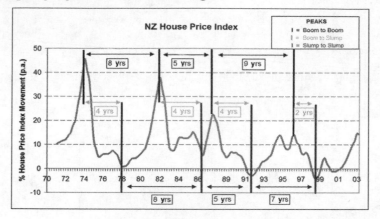

Graph A.1

Key Driver Peaks and Troughs

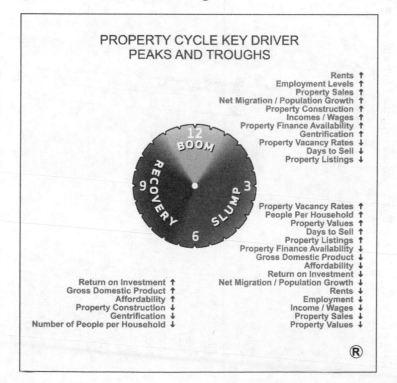

List of All Key Driver Peaks and Troughs Throughout a Complete Cycle

	RECOVERY			BOOM			SLUMP		
	Beginning	Middle	End	Beginning	Middle	End	Beginning	Middle	End
DEMOGRAPHIC									
Net Migration/Population Growth	+	+	+	+	Peak	–	–	Trough	+
Property Vacancy Rates	–	–	–	–	–	Trough	+	Peak	–
Employment	+	+	+	+	+	Peak	–	–	Trough
Property Construction	Trough	+	+	+	+	Peak	–	–	–
No. of People per Household	–	Trough	+	+	+	+	Peak	–	–
FINANCIAL									
Property ROI	+	Peak	–	–	–	–	–	Trough	+
Rents	+	+	+	+	Peak	–	–	–	Trough
Incomes	+	+	+	+	+	Peak	–	–	Trough
Property Finance Availability	+	Peak	+	+	+	Peak	–	–	Trough
Gross Domestic Product	+	Peak	–	–	–	–	Trough	+	+
Property Values	+	+	+	+	+	+	Peak	–	Trough
Property Affordability	Peak	–	–	–	–	–	Trough	+	+
EMOTIONAL									
No. of Days To Sell Property	–	–	–	–	–	Trough	+	+	Peak
Gentrification	Trough	+	+	+	+	Peak	–	–	–
Property Listings	–	–	–	–	Trough	+	+	+	Peak
Property Sales	+	+	+	+	Peak	–	–	–	Trough

Key

Peak	=	When a key driver is at its highest point, just before it begins to decline
Trough	=	When a key diver is at its lowest point, just before it begins to rise
+	=	Increase in key driver
–	=	Decrease in key driver
ROI	=	Return on investment

Key Drivers

In the key driver graphs the thin line represents the annualised house price index percentage change (left-hand scale) and the thick line represents the annualised percentage change in the key driver (right-hand scale). Each peak is identified with a grey circle and a grey arrow points to the year in which the peak occurred. Each trough is identified with a black circle and a black arrow points to the year in which the trough occurred.

Demographic

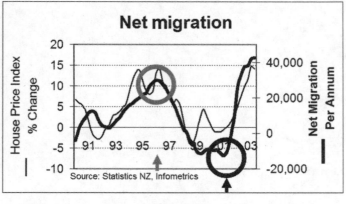

Graph A.2

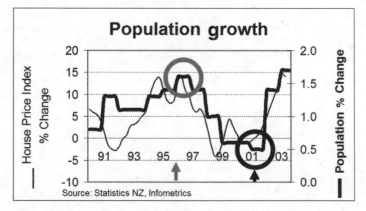

Graph A.3

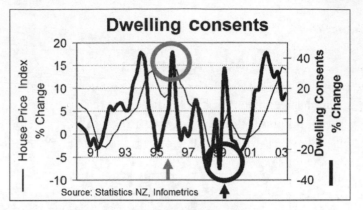

Graph A.4

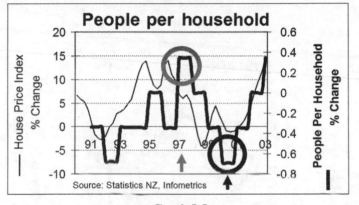

Graph A.5

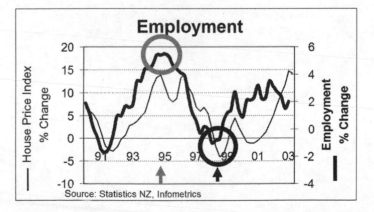

Graph A.6

Financial

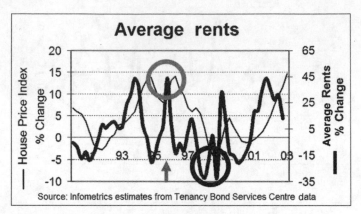

Graph A.7

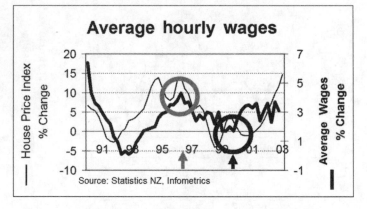

Graph A.8

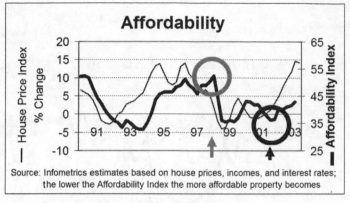

Graph A.9

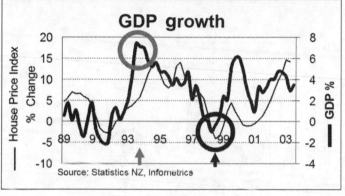

Graph A.10

Emotional

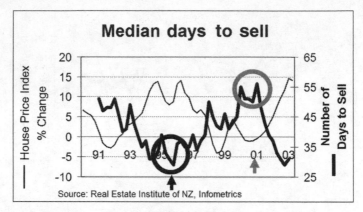

Graph A.11

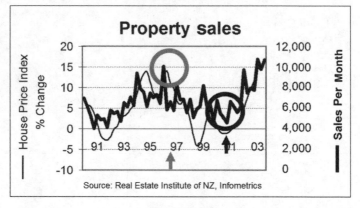

Graph A.12

Market Influencers

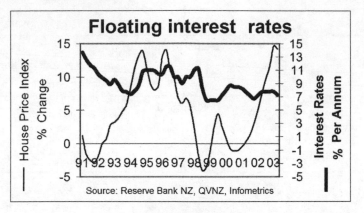

Graph A.13

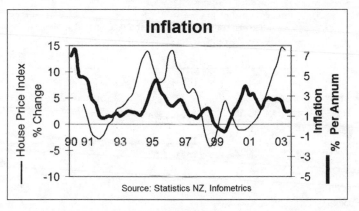

Graph A.14

Peaks and Troughs of Key Drivers during the Recovery

Peak	*Trough*
Demographic	
	Property Construction
	No. of People per Household
Financial	
Return on Investment	
Gross Domestic Product	
Property Affordability	
Emotional	
	Gentrification

Peaks and Troughs of Key Drivers during the Boom

Peak	*Trough*
Demographic	
Property Construction	Property Vacancy Rates
Net Migration / Population	
Employment	
Financial	
Rents	
Incomes	
Property Finance Availability	
Emotional	
Property Sales	Property Listings
Gentrification	No. of Days to Sell Property

Peaks and Troughs of Key Drivers during the Slump

Peak	*Trough*
Demographic	
Property Vacancy Rates	Net Migration/Population
No. of People per Household	Employment
Financial	
Property Value Growth	Property Value Growth
	Return on Investment
	Rents
	Incomes
	Property Affordability
	Property Finance Availability
	Goss Domestic Product
Emotional	
No. of Days to Sell Property	Property Sales
Property Listings	

Endnotes

1. *100 Years of Land Values in Chicago* by Homer Hoyt, reprinted 2000 by Beard Books, Washington D.C.
2. Richard Reed of Melbourne University.

Disclaimer

Kieran Trass, the Hybrid Group Limited and the Hybrid Group of companies (Hybrid Group) does not intend for the information contained in this book to be used as a substitute for personalsied investment advice. We recommend that you seek the advice of professional financial, taxation and legal advisors before entering into any financial transaction or making any investment decision.

Disclosure of Interest

Kieran Trass, the directors, officers, commission agents, consultants and employees of the Hybrid Group advise that they and persons associated with them may have an interest in any properties, products or services offered by them, and that they may earn commissions, fees and other benefits and advantages, whether pecuniary or not and whether direct or indirect, in connection with the making of a recommendation or any dealing by a client in these properties, products or services.

The Hybrid
Group Story

The Hybrid Group Story

by Kieran Trass

The Hybrid Group of companies began and has evolved as a direct result of the needs of residential property investors.

As a property investor, while working in the finance industry, I found that getting the right finance structure was critical to enable the growth of any property portfolio. Because every investor had a unique set of financial circumstances I learned that it was critical to tailor suitable funding solutions to each individual's financial circumstances. In 1996 I established the Hybrid Group, New Zealand's first dedicated property investment mortgage broking firm, to provide specialist advice on how to 'mortgage yourself to wealth'.

Over the following few years I found many investors using different strategies to grow their property portfolios. But I found some investors seemed to achieve far more than others even though they had similar financial circumstances. Some used a methodical plan to grow their portfolio in order to achieve predetermined goals, but most didn't. I found I spent more and more of my time giving advice to investors on creating a plan for the growth of their portfolio and setting goals based on their specific circumstances. This led to the need for further advice on how to achieve that plan by defining what properties they should buy, how they should make offers, when they should buy specific types of properties and where they should buy properties to maximise the growth of their portfolio.

So out of this need the Hybrid Group started offering *property investment advisory services*. Clients immediately welcomed the service as it catered perfectly to their needs.

Once our clients had a property investment plan, they wanted to know what factors influenced the local property market and what opportunities might eventuate as a result.

So out of this need the Hybrid Group started offering the *property cycle commentary*. Clients immediately welcomed this service as it complemented their ability to achieve their plan.

Now our clients could access the right finance structure, they had a property investment plan and they knew how they would achieve it. But then we found many clients didn't have the time to look for suitable properties to purchase.

So out of this need the Hybrid Group commenced its *property dealing business* to source good SAFE property deals. Clients immediately saw the value of this service as it saved them the time-consuming task of having to source good property deals.

With the advent of modern legal entities such as family trusts, loss attributing qualifying companies and the like, more and more clients started to seek our advice about suitable structures to protect their assets without jeopardising their tax position.

So out of this need Hybrid Group commenced its *asset protection business* with a well-qualified in-house lawyer to advise clients on what structures they should use and then to put those structures in place.

As the property cycle progressed, in 2002–03 we entered the boom phase of the property cycle. Our clients found it harder to find strong cashflow properties.

In response to this Hybrid Group recognised the opportunity to generate a strong cashflow by adding extra dwellings on single-dwelling land which was allowed to have more than one dwelling on it.

So out of this need Hybrid Group commenced its turnkey *rental dwelling construction company*. Within a short time, dozens of properties were being constructed for our clients.

With the complexity of tax laws relating to depreciation, more and more of our clients sought clarification from us about how to appraise the fit out, chattels and fittings value of their buildings.

So out of this need Hybrid Group commenced its *chattels appraisal business* with a well-designed system to accurately estimate the value of fit out, chattels and fittings of rental properties.

As our clients' knowledge and understanding of the property market and the property cycle grew, more and more of them expressed a need for accurate capital growth statistics for various city suburbs. They had found that medians and averages often quoted in the media were open to distortion and were not a true representation of what was really happening to property prices.

So out of this need the Hybrid Group approached Quotable Value to assist with the creation of a new index to more accurately measure property price growth within specific areas of cities. This resulted in the creation of the Hybrid Capital Growth Index (HCGI) to measure historical property prices and to help forecast future price movements. The HCGI is used to produce the *Hybrid Capital Growth Reports.*

Over the years many property investors have sought our advice about chartered accountants. Many clients expressed their dissatisfaction with the quality and high cost of advice from their accountants as well as the length of time it took to deliver financial statements and accounts.

So out of this need Hybrid Group is commencing its accounting business to provide *specialised property investment accounting advice* combined with well-designed systems and procedures to quickly and competently produce financial statements and accounts for property investors.

The Hybrid Group story continues to evolve, but at the core of all of the Hybrid Group's activities has always been the needs of residential property investors. Expect new and innovative services to continue to be driven by those needs.

Hybrid Group Services

Hybrid Mortgage Consulting

- Providing the rocket fuel to propel your property portfolio to new heights!

- Mortgage broking and property portfolio consulting systems including our unique Interest Rate Averaging system.

- Property Cycle Survival Pack which includes property portfolio analysis and recommendations.

Hybrid Property Sourcing

- Giving you back your weekends! You don't have to spend your weekends trying to source good property deals because we do it for you.

- We find and buy the best deals and then give you the opportunity to buy them from us!

Hybrid Dwellings

- We build cash registers on your land!

- Turn your spare land into a cash-generating asset with the construction of a purpose-designed rental property.

- We can take care of the complete project for you.

Hybrid Chattels Appraisals

- Generate more cashflow by maximising your legitimate tax deductions!

- Make sure you get the depreciation you are entitled to with our professional and systems-driven appraisal service.

Hybrid Accounting

- You don't have to wait six months to get your financial accounts back from your accountant any more!

- We make sure you receive your financials quickly combined with the quality of service you deserve as a property investor.

For further details on the services of the Hybrid Group Ltd visit **www.hybridgroup.co.nz** plus access these online innovations coming soon:

1. *Property Cycle Commentary*
   - New Zealand Property Cycle Commentary

2. *New Zealand Capital Growth Reports*
   - Auckland Regions
   - Wellington Regions
   - Christchurch Regions
   - Forecast Hot Spot Reports

3. *International Property Cycle Commentaries*
   - Australia
   - USA
   - UK
   - Plus more . . .

INFOMETRICS

Since being founded in 1983
Infometrics has built a reputation for rigorous
and independent economic consulting
and forecasting services.

Infometrics Property is a subscription website providing approximately twenty-five data series for seventy areas around New Zealand, including some of the key drivers for the real estate market highlighted in *Grow Rich with the Property Cycle*.

The site also gives subscribers:

- analysis of the property sector by Infometrics economists

- commentary on interest rates

- links to a collection of recent news stories from the housing market to keep you informed on the latest real estate developments.

Infometrics' other subscription services include:

- economic forecasts – analysis of household income and expenditure, business investment, financial data including interest rate and exchange rate forecasts, monetary and fiscal policy developments, and external trade trends

- building and property forecasts – containing an economic forecast summary, population and demographic trends, house sales and prices, residential building activity, trends in non-residential property, and non-residential building activity

- transport forecasts – containing an economic forecast summary, a review of air, rail, road and shipping activity, trends in transport prices, car and truck sales, key sectors relevant to transport activity, and a calendar of key events in the vehicle industry.

Forecasts are published three times per year. Subscribers to the forecasts also get access to Infometrics' website – updated every week with analysis on the latest economic data, trends and issues.

To subscribe, or for more information on any of Infometrics' services, visit **www.infometrics.co.nz**, or email **economics@infometrics.co.nz**.

The Hybrid Real Estate Board Game

Experience is usually something you get just after you need it most!

But now you can experience the complete Property Cycle in just a few fun hours!

Kieran Trass designed this unique game to teach you the strategies of how to grow a long-term property portfolio in spite of the impacts of the property cycle . . .

Play this educational board game and you can learn:

- how you can read the property cycle like a book
- how you can use property to make a fortune with a sustainable income stream
- how to keep that fortune even in a property downturn

This game is the most fun and relevant platform for you to practise your way to property wealth. This challenging and educational board game brings you Edutainment (education through entertainment). Developed specifically to mirror the trials of building a property portfolio in real life, and to educate you about the typical property cycle, this board game offers a powerful way to practise building a property portfolio to achieve financial freedom so you never have to work again.

Compelling Benefits You Will Enjoy From This Unique Property Board Game!

1. Learn how to achieve your property investment goals.

2. Invest time learning about your big-picture property investment strategy.

3. Learn to consider property opportunities in view of your long-term goals.

4. Learn to watch the property cycle while considering opportunities.

5. Learn the true cost of distractions while you try to build your portfolio.

6. Learn to stay focused on your progress.

7. Learn how to track your goal progress.

8. Teach your family and friends how to succeed in property investment too.

9. Learn about the factors impacting on the property cycle.

10. Learn to focus on the numbers that really count.

11. Learn some of the mistakes of property investing without making them in real life.

12. Learn when the optimum times to buy are imminent.

13. Learn to balance your financial resources to grow your property portfolio.

14. Learn to achieve realistic financial goals irrespective of what your income is.

15. Stay in front of the pack of other investors by increasing your knowledge.

15. Accelerate your learning curve by interacting with other players.

16. Plus so much more you will be amazed!

Testimonials

Hybrid Real Estate Board Game

'What an amazing game – gave me a safe environment to play with numbers and get a better handle on how important they are. Anybody who is serious about property investing needs to be exposed to this game.' *MG*

'Very educational. Will help for own goals in property investing.' *GJM*

'Wow, I've learnt just as much from watching the other players as with my own game. Interesting to see my reaction to changes. Learnt lots. Excellent game.' *CM*

'Helps one focus in a non-threatening environment on the specific rewards, risks and challenges of residential property investment.' *GP*

'Encourages one to think ahead and highlights the dangers in the market.' *CM*

'Definitely a great learning tool and a good way to see the property cycle in action.' *CD*

'Playing the game increased my confidence in my ability to build a safe and profitable residential investment portfolio.' *GF*

'Teaches you how to balance equity and passive cashflow.' *DA*

'Teaches you that property investment is a marathon, not a sprint.' *WF*

'A fun interactive game that takes you through the highs and lows associated with property investments!' *NB*

'Good learning experience and a cheap way to make mistakes.' *MM*

'Valuable insight into each facet of the property cycle.' *BD*

'Good simulation of what happens in real life.' *RD*

WARNING: READ THIS FINE PRINT!

The Hybrid Real Estate Board Game is a powerful and exciting game which can influence or increase your desire to play the game of property investment in real life! This game could affect your future property purchasing decisions and may result in you achieving financial freedom sooner.

Purchase the **HYBRID REAL ESTATE BOARD GAME** at your bookseller, or order online now at **www.hybridgroup.co.nz** or FAX the order form on the following page to New Zealand (09) 638-3351.

1. **N.B. FOR ALL OFFSHORE ORDERS**
   No GST applies but a purchase price premium of 12.5% is charged.

2. Games are air-freighted only and attract the following P&P charges:

   anywhere in NZ $20;

   Australia NZ$70;

   other International NZ$130.

Price for all orders:

NZ$99.95 plus Freight Charge (includes GST in NZ).

Contact Details:

First Name: _____

Last Name: _____

Email Address: _____

Phone: _____

Physical Address: _____

Suburb: _____

City: _____

Postcode: _____

State: _____

Country: _____

Payment Details:

Card Type: _____ VISA / MASTERCARD / AMEX _____

Card Holder: _____

Card Number: _____

Card Expiry: _____

❏ I confirm that I am the cardholder and agree that my credit card
   will be charged for the game and any applicable freight on receipt
   of order.

....

- Please allow 2–3 weeks for delivery on receipt of this order.

- We cannot deliver to P.O. Boxes.

- While every endeavour will be made to deliver your game undamaged it is
  possible that minor box damage may occur during freighting.